To:

From:

⊰ 52 ⊱
NAMES OF GOD IN
HEBREW

EVERY CHRISTIAN
SHOULD KNOW

Dave Adamson

Christian Art
PUBLISHERS

Visit Christian Art Gifts, Inc., at www.christianartgifts.com.

52 Names of God in Hebrew Every Christian Should Know

Published by Christian Art Gifts, Inc., Bloomingdale, IL, USA.

© 2024 by Dave Adamson. All rights reserved.

First edition.

The author is represented by Kobus Johnsen of Johnsen Inc.

Designed by Brad Miedema.

Cover and interior images used under license from the author and Shutterstock.com.

ISBN 978-1-63952-725-0

Printed in China.

30 29 28 27 26 25
12 11 10 9 8 7 6 5 4 3

FOR THE PEOPLE WHO ENGAGE
WITH MY DAILY DEVOTIONAL POSTS
ON INSTAGRAM AND MY READING PLANS
ON THE YOUVERSION BIBLE APP—
MAY THIS BE ANOTHER RESOURCE
TO HELP YOU TAKE THE NEXT STEP IN
YOUR FAITH JOURNEY WITH JESUS.

AND TO PAUL RUDD,
MY THIRD-FAVORITE JEWISH MAN.

CONTENTS

How to use this book? 11

1. **Ab** (Father) 13

2. **Elohim** (God) 15

3. **Yahweh Roi** (The Lord, My Shepherd) 17

4. **Yahweh Meqaddishkem** (The Lord Who Sanctifies You) 19

5. **Yahweh Nissi** (The Lord My Banner) 21

6. **Yahweh Shalom** (Lord of Peace) 23

7. **Ehyeh Asher Ehyeh** (I Am That I Am) 25

8. **El Roi** (The God Who Sees Me) 27

9. **Aleph Tav** (Beginning and End) 29

10. **Yeshua** (Salvation) 31

11. **Davar** (The Word) 33

12. **Mayim Chayyim** (Living Water) 35

13. **Ro'eh tzon** (Shepherd of a Flock) 37

14. **Ruach HaKodesh** (Holy Spirit) 39

15. **El Shaddai** (Lord God Almighty) 41

CONTENTS

16. **El Elyon** (God Most High) 43

17. **Yahweh Sabaoth** (The Lord of Hosts) 45

18. **El Hakkavod** (The God of Glory) 47

19. **Yahweh Tsidkenu** (The Lord Is Our Righteousness) 49

20. **El Gibbor** (The Mighty God) 51

21. **Atik Yomin** (Ancient of Days) 53

22. **Yahweh** (Lord) 55

23. **El Olam** (The Everlasting God) 57

24. **Yahweh Rophe** (The Lord Heals) 59

25. **El Kannah** (Jealous God) 61

26. **Esh Okelah** (Consuming Fire) 63

27. **Yahweh Jireh** (The Lord Will Provide) 65

28. **Qedosh Yisra'el** (Holy One of Israel) 67

29. **Shekinah** (The Presence of God) 69

30. **Yahweh Tsuri** (The Lord Is My Rock) 71

31. **Yahweh Shammah** (The Lord Is There) 73

CONTENTS

32. **Boker Lo Avot** (Morning Without Clouds) 75

33. **Yahweh Magen** (God Is My Shield) 77

34. **Migdal-Oz** (Strong Tower or Fortress) 79

35. **Melek** (King) 81

36. **Elohei Ma'uzzi** (God of My Strength) 83

37. **El Echad** (The One God) 85

38. **Yatsar** (The Creator) 87

39. **Yahweh Chesed** (God of Loyal Love) 89

40. **Emmanuel** (God with Us) 91

41. **El Channun** (The Gracious God) 93

42. **El Hanne'eman** (The Faithful God) 95

43. **El Bethel** (God of the House of God) 97

44. **Adon ha'adonim** (Lord of Lords) 99

45. **Ohr HaOlam** (Light of the World) 101

46. **Sar Shalom** (Prince of Peace) 103

CONTENTS

47. **Lechem Ha-Chayim** (Bread of Life) 105

48. **Mashiach** (Messiah) 107

49. **Goel** (Redeemer) 109

50. **Rabbi** (Teacher) 111

51. **Nechama** (God of All Comfort) 113

52. **Seh HaElohim** (Lamb of God) 115

HOW TO USE THIS BOOK

When you set out to write a book outlining "fifty-two names for God in Hebrew," there are a number of factors that shape the work.

First, the number of names for God found throughout the Bible numbers a lot more than fifty-two, so choosing the fifty-two you want to cover is subjective. Second, you have to decide if you're covering only the names of God found in the Hebrew Scriptures (what many followers of Jesus refer to as the Old Testament), or if you're also including the names for Jesus found in the Christian Scriptures (Old and New Testament). If you do decide to include the names for Jesus, which were probably Greek names since this was the language used by the authors of this part of the Bible, should you translate them from Greek to Hebrew to English for the purpose of a book like this?

Once you land on a position on these two issues, you then need to work out how you will translate the Hebrew into English. Typically, Hebrew words are transliterated phonetically, which means the spelling of certain words will vary.

These are just some of the factors that need to be considered when writing this type of book, and why I want to state up front that this book is not the ultimate guide to translating Hebrew into English. This is a devotional book, not an academic paper on Biblical Hebrew. I have made every attempt to use multiple sources to research the content, meeting with rabbinic friends to discuss background and pastoral friends to provide practical applications. I hope the result is a book that will inspire, inform, and encourage.

I would like to thank the many rabbis, pastors, scholars, and mentors who have helped increase my understanding of Hebrew culture, and especially Michael and Vanessa, Gabby, Travis, Kayla, Kenji, David and all my friends at The Fellow of Israel Related Ministries (FIRM) for their support and inspiration. (If you would like to transform lives in Israel through gospel-centered ministries, go to firmisrael.org.) I would also like to thank Kobus Johnsen for his suggestion to write this book in the first place. Thanks, mate!

Finally, I need to thank my wife, Meg; and our three daughters, Chelsea, Ella, and Jordyn. You guys are simply the best.

אב

FATHER

ƎB
FATHER

What is childlike faith?

Do you know what it means to have faith like a child?

Sometimes when I go out to take sunrise photos, I take my daughters with me. I remember one time, as I stood in amazement watching a spectacular sunrise, my youngest daughter stood next to me with her arms crossed, complaining about being outside when she wanted to go home to watch TV. I was experiencing childlike awe; she was having a childish tantrum.

There's a big difference between child*ish* and child*like*.

Jesus once told his followers that to be part of God's kingdom, they needed to have "childlike" faith. Childlike faith is filled with awe and wonder. It believes anything is possible. It trusts. It's curious. It's resilient and fearless.

What I love about this idea of "childlike" faith is that it places God in the position of Father. The Hebrew word we translate as "father" throughout Scripture is *ab* (אב, pronounced "av")—which can refer to someone who becomes a father naturally or through adoption. Interestingly, most Christians assume the Hebrew word for father is *abba*, but this is Aramaic.

Now, I realize that as our faith matures, it's hard to hold on to the childlike awe and curiosity that places God in the position of Father. Childlike faith is often impacted by our adult questions about such things as Scripture, faith, and life. Author Bob Goff offers the antidote to this: "When you feel like you can't explain your faith, go love someone." That's childlike simplicity.

Simply loving and accepting the people around us can make faith a lot less complicated—for us *and* them!

So, are you ready to have childlike faith by loving the people around you?

"Truly I tell you, unless you change and become like little children, you will never enter the kingdom of heaven." — Matthew 18:3

אלהים

GOD

ELOHIM
GOD

Do you know God's most-used name?

God is called by many names in the Bible, but one of the most often used is *Elohim* (אלהים, pronounced "eh-lo-heem"), which means a range of things including "mighty" or "powerful," "divine," "supreme," "great," and "God."

Elohim appears more than 2,500 times in the Bible.

In fact, this word *Elohim*, which appears in the very first line of the Bible, is interesting because in Hebrew it is the plural form of the word *God*, which is *El*. So, this means the oldest name of God actually means "Gods," which followers of Jesus will recognize as a hint of the Trinity in the first verse of the Bible!

And because the first mention of this name in the Bible is paired with the Hebrew word *bara* (ברא, pronounced "bah-rah"), which means "he created," the word *Elohim* contains the idea that God is the Creator. I think that's why so many people experience God in nature.

If you have ever had a sense of awe when you're at the beach or looking at the stars in the night sky, then you're experiencing this *Elohim*. I remember the first time I ever saw Yosemite Valley, just after a snowstorm. I was overwhelmed by the creative power of God. It was truly breathtaking

But I think the most significant part of God being the Creator is that it means God created you. While *Elohim* created the Milky Way, the waves in the ocean, El Capitan, and Half Dome, the pinnacle of His creativity was you.

You were created by God as an expression of his wisdom and goodness. And if that wasn't enough, I believe you were created for a reason. In Jeremiah 29:11, God says he knows the plans he has for you, and those plans include a good future filled with hope.

So, since all the awe and wonder and magnificence of the Divine Creator has been placed in you on purpose, what will you do today?

How will you be an expression of the awesomeness of *Elohim*?

In the beginning God created the heavens and the earth. — Genesis 1:1

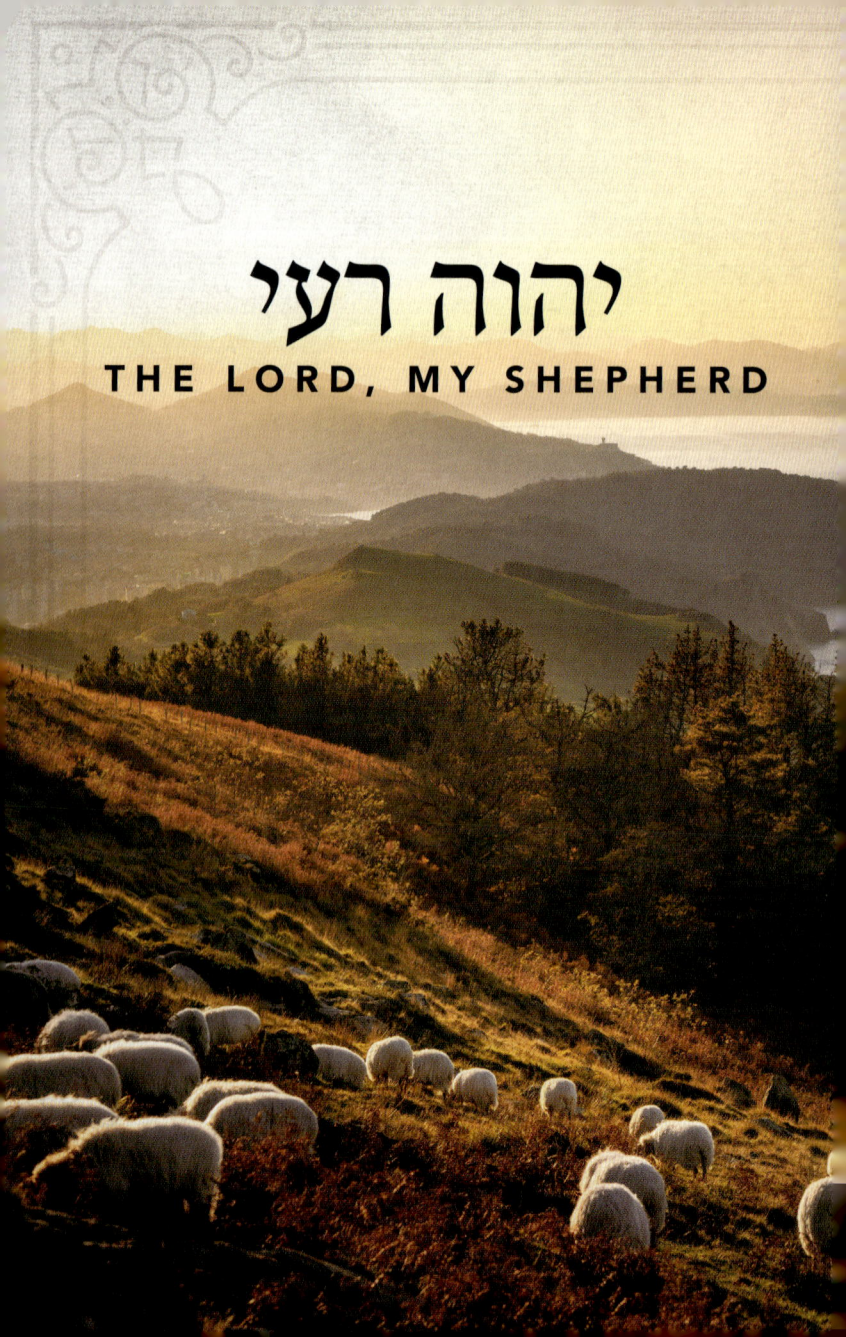

YAHWEH ROI
THE LORD, MY SHEPHERD

Where is God when life is darkest?

There are a lot of shepherd images throughout the Bible, but the most well-known is found in Psalm 23. This poem has deepened my faith more than any other, but only after I learned what it meant to be a shepherd in Israel.

See, in Australia where I'm from, sheep are moved by trained dogs barking at them and herding them from behind. But in Israel, it's a shepherd who leads the sheep.

During the day, the shepherd walks in front of the flock, leading them with the sound of his voice. The sheep know their shepherd's voice and follow, just like in the opening of Psalm 23, which reads, "He *leads* me beside quiet waters" (Psalm 23:2, emphasis added).

But when the sun goes down in the desert, I've seen first-hand how a shepherd moves into the middle of the flock so they can stand amongst the sheep to guide them. And this is when God lives up to the name given to Him by David: The Lord Is My Shepherd.

The sheep move forward safely, knowing their shepherd is right beside them when it's dark. Just as the psalmist writes, "I will not be afraid, for you are close *beside* me. Your rod and your staff protect and comfort me." (Psalm 23:4 NLT, emphasis added).

You see, when life is darkest, God is closest.

And the Hebrew word we translate as "staff" in this verse is *mishenet* (משענת, pronounced "mish-eh-net"), which means "a support." It means that when life is darkest, God is beside us to support us. When your life is darkest, God is the Good Shepherd who supports and comforts you and is beside you.

If you're reading these words and are walking through a dark valley today, I believe God wants to remind you that He is with you right now.

I will not be afraid, for you are close beside me. — Psalm 23:4 NLT

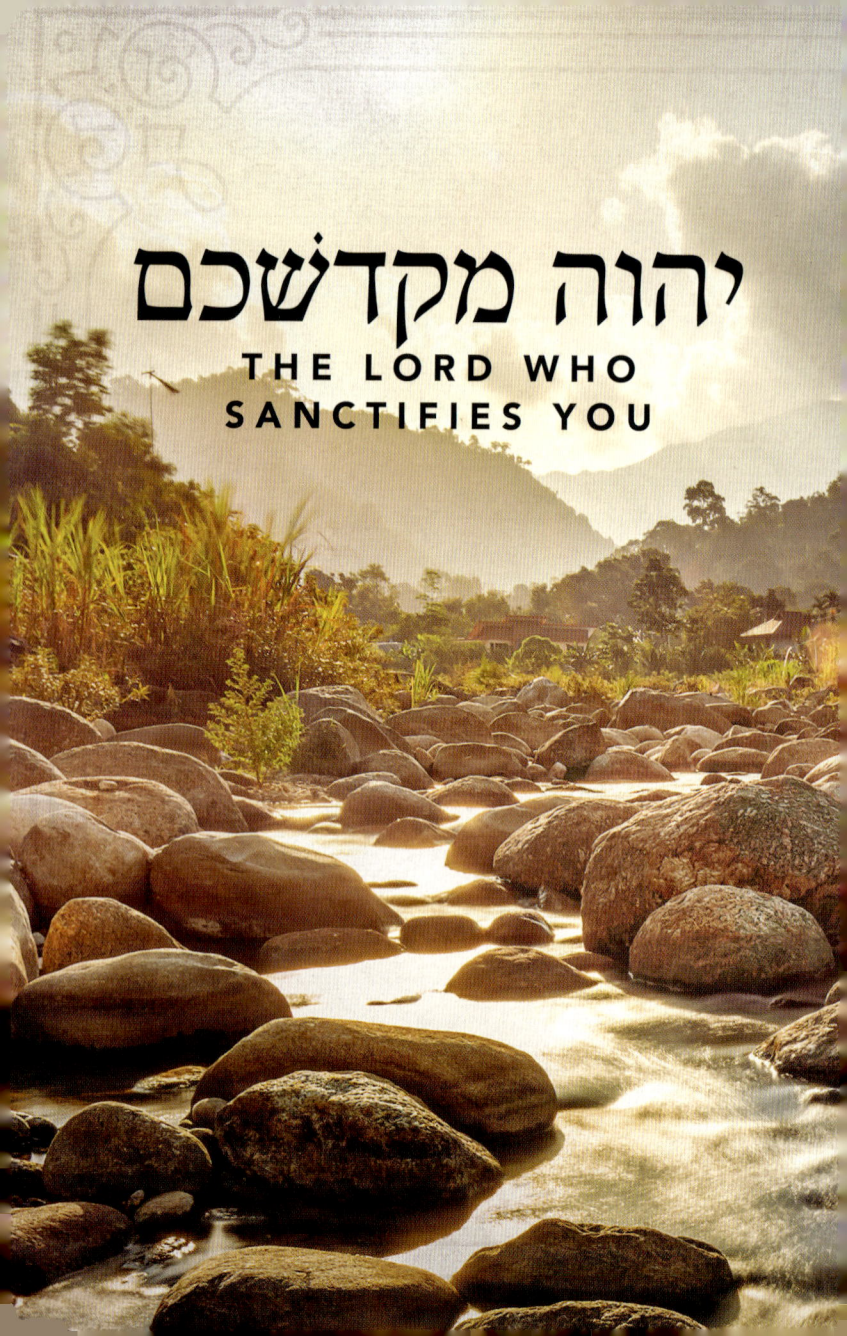

YAHWEH MEQADDISHKEM
THE LORD WHO SANCTIFIES YOU

What is God's purpose for you?

When I first started following Jesus, people told me that God had a plan and purpose for everyone who believed in Him. Naturally, I wanted to find out what that was for me—and it turned out the answer was in one of the names of God!

That name is *Yahweh Meqaddishkem* in Hebrew (יהוה מקדשכם, pronounced "Yah-weh me-qad-dish-kem"), which translates into English as "The Lord Who Sanctifies You." This literally means that God sets you apart to be holy.

Now, *sanctification* is one of those words you only ever hear in church or read in the Bible, but it's essentially just a big word for becoming more like Jesus.

Put another way, sanctification is the process of God helping you to become who He truly created you to be.

That's God's plan for you!

Becoming more like Jesus means that God works in you to help you care for and serve others like Jesus did. He helps you to encourage, pray, speak, and act like Jesus.

I believe being more like Jesus means loving the "unlovable," forgiving the "unworthy," showing compassion and mercy to those in need, and doing good for people who will never be able to repay you.

However, it's important to remember that this is a process. It doesn't happen overnight; it requires a lifetime. And it also requires you to be willing to cooperate with what God wants for you and your life. It requires full obedience. Your obedience will produce a miracle that you cannot get on your own. *That's* sanctification!

Just imagine what the world would be like if everyone who followed Jesus were more like Jesus!

It is God's will that you should be sanctified. — 1 Thessalonians 4:3

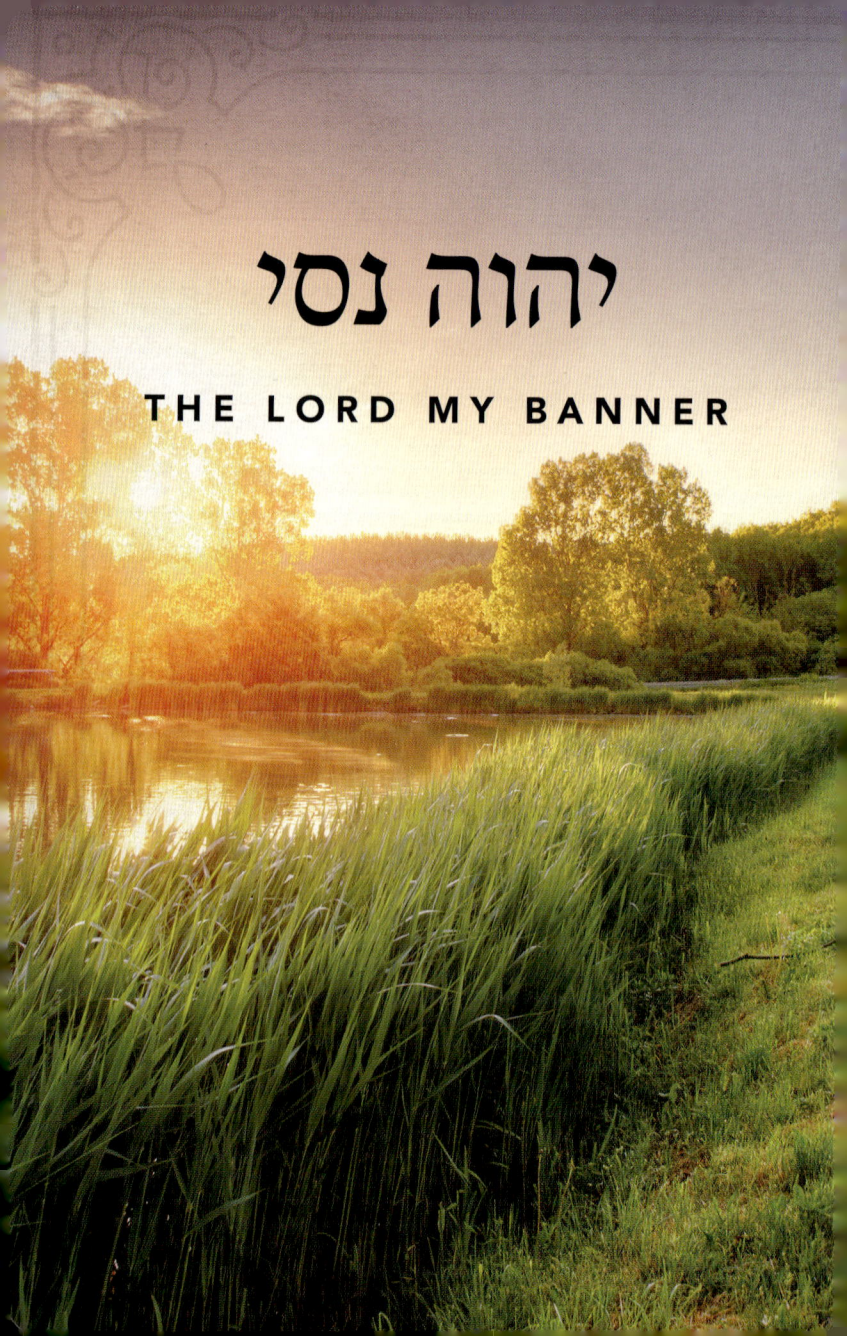

יהוה נסי

THE LORD MY BANNER

ɣAႹWEႹ NISSI
THE LORD MY BANNER

Where is God in hard times?

Many of us have probably wondered where God was when we faced a tough situation or life was not going as expected. Maybe you've found yourself asking this question recently.

This is when one of the Hebrew names for God gives me hope. The name is *Yahweh Nissi* (יהוה נסי, pronounced "Yah-weh nis-see"), which means "The Lord My Banner."

Moses gave God this name in the book of Exodus after the Lord had helped the Israelites win a battle in the middle of the wilderness. During the victory celebration, Moses built an altar to God and called it *Yahweh Nissi*—the Lord My Banner.

A banner is a flag or symbol that represents hope and purpose. So, what battles are you facing today where you could use some hope and purpose?

Perhaps you are facing sickness or disease. Maybe you are facing an uphill battle in your marriage. Maybe you have lost a job. Or perhaps you are desperate to restore a relationship.

Whatever battle you are facing, I believe *Yahweh Nissi* wants to remind you of three truths today:

1. When God is your banner, He will sustain you. You might feel like you're not going to make it, but God promises to provide you with what you need. It may not be what you want, but it will be what you need to be obedient to him.
2. When God is your banner, His purpose will prevail. If your circumstance is causing you to lose faith, "fix your eyes on Jesus" (Heb. 12:2) and His purpose, and you will be able to stand strong.
3. When God is your banner, He is always with you. God promises to walk with you through every situation. You are never alone.

If you're in a battle right now, remember that Jesus is your banner who brings hope and purpose.

Moses built an altar there and named it Yahweh-Nissi (which means "the LORD is my banner"). — Exodus 17:15 NLT

יהוה שלום

LORD OF PEACE

ΥΛΠWEΠ SHΛLOM
LORD OF PEACE

Is your life hard right now?

Wouldn't it be awesome if when you started following Jesus, all your problems, stresses, and fears simply disappeared forever?

Sure, that seems great, but it's not what we're promised anywhere in Scripture. God never promises to remove all the hard times in life; rather, He promises to walk with us through them. This is when He lives up to his name of being the Lord of Peace.

Many of the authors of the Bible use the title "Lord of Peace" when referring to God. In Hebrew, "Lord of Peace" is translated as *Yahweh Shalom* (יהוה שלום, pronounced "Yah-weh shah-lome"), which can be translated as "the Lord is complete" or "the Lord brings security." Yes, it refers to God being able to calm the storms in life, but it's more about His ability to give us everything we need to get *through* life.

When we walk through troubled waters, we don't have to drown, because God offers us complete security.

As C. S. Lewis once wrote, "Life with God is not immunity from difficulties, but peace in difficulties." His point is that God is everything we need to get through the hard times we all face.

Author Sadie Robinson puts it this way: "It's not that things aren't going to get scary, it's when you're in the face of fear you carry peace…knowing you have victory because your God is bigger." I love that!

God is enough for you to find complete peace and security in the chaos of your situation because He is the Lord of Peace!

Only God, the Lord of Peace, can bring hope where there is hopelessness, light where there is darkness, and peace where there is anxiety.

Can I get an "Amen!"?

"Peace I leave with you; my peace I give you. I do not give to you as the world gives. Do not let your hearts be troubled and do not be afraid."
— John 14:27

EHYEH
ASHER EHYEH
I AM THAT I AM

One of God's names is "I AM," but do you know what this name means?

When we are introduced to someone new, we might ask their name, right? But when Moses asked about God's name in the famous story of the burning bush, he didn't say, "What is your name?" More accurately, he asked God, "What is the significance of your name?" Let me explain.

In Hebrew, Moses asked, "*mah shemo*" (מה שמו, pronounced "Mah-shemo, which means "what does your name mean?" And God answered the question by saying, "I AM That I AM." In Hebrew, this is the phrase *Ehyeh Asher Ehyeh* (אהיה אשר אהיה, pronounced "eh-yeh a-share eh-yeh"), which can be translated several ways including "I exist," or "I will exist," or "I will be," or even "I am who I will be."

God was making the point that He is the God who was, who is, and who will always be—He does not change. God is constant.

In the same way we can count on the sun to come up every morning, we can count on God to be consistent.

And the significance of this for us is that all the character traits and attributes God has in the Bible are what He still has today. As author John Mark Comer reminds us, "God's name is a stand-in for his character."

So, because we know God had compassion in the time of the Bible, we can be confident He will have compassion for us today.

If God showed generous mercy to His people then, He will show generous mercy to you today.

God rescued His people then, so He can and will rescue you today.

No matter what situation you're currently facing, God's name reminds you that because He came through for His people in the past, He will come through for you in the present.

As Dr. Tony Evans says, "God's name covers all: past, present, and future. He's got you covered."

God said to Moses, "I AM WHO I AM." And he said, "Say this to the people of Israel: 'I AM has sent me to you.'" — Exodus 3:14 ESV

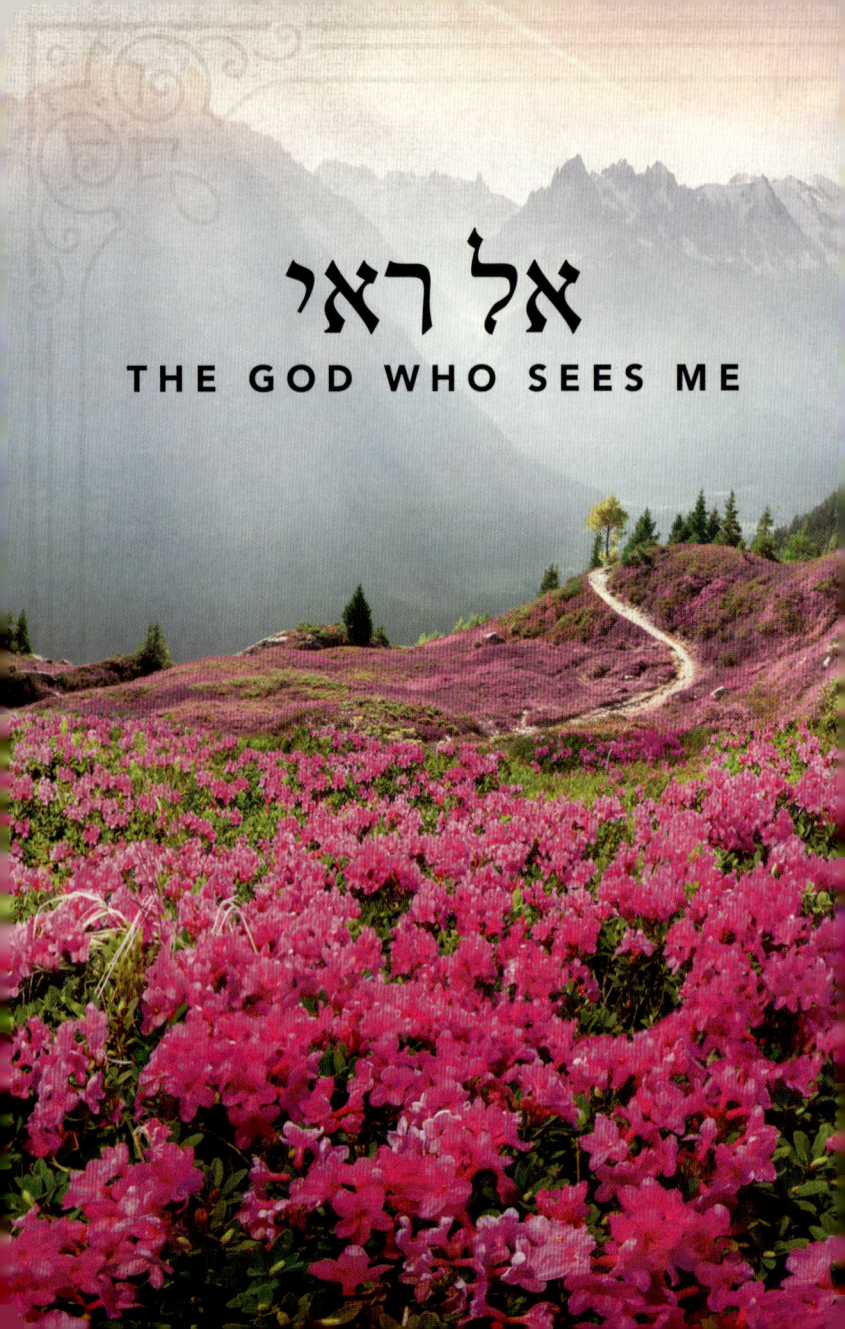

EL ROI
THE GOD WHO SEES ME

Does God even notice you?

I think one of the most comforting names of God is found in Genesis 16:13 when Hagar, an Egyptian slave from Abraham's house, describes God as "the God who sees me."

In Hebrew, this name is *El Roi* (אל ראי, pronounced "el-ro-ee"), which literally translates as "The God Who Sees Me."

I think this is comforting because it's a reminder that God sees everything. He knows your past, your present, and your future.

When Hagar referred to God as *El Roi*, it gave her comfort to know that God was with her, watching over her and assuring her of His promises.

For me, it's a reminder that God sees everything I'm facing, everything I'm going through, and is ready to help me get through hard times.

It's also a reminder that when God looks at *you*, He sees the beauty He created and His purposes for you.

He doesn't just see an enneagram number, a personality color, or a series of Myers-Briggs letters, because you're so much more than that. He sees his "workmanship" (Ephesians 2:10 ESV).

When God looks at you, He sees his son or daughter. He sees a person who has been "wonderfully made" (Psalm 139:14) with "imperishable beauty" (1 Peter 3:4 ESV).

When God looks at you, He sees a person worth dying for. Which is, of course, exactly what He did!

She gave this name to the LORD who spoke to her: "You are the God who sees me," for she said, "I have now seen the One who sees me."
— Genesis 16:13

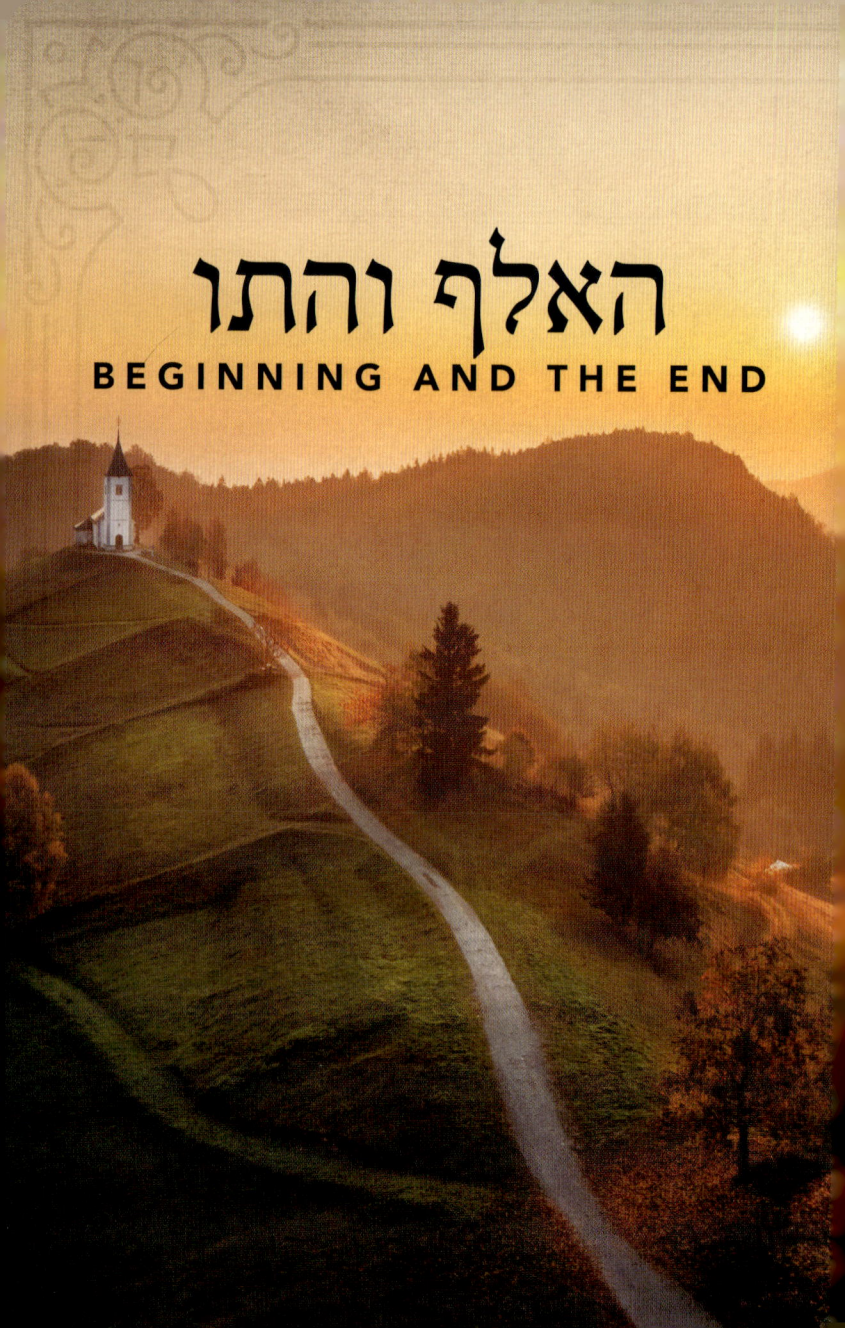

האלף והתו

BEGINNING AND THE END

ALEPH TAV
BEGINNING AND THE END

Every photographer knows that the best times to shoot outdoors are at the beginning and the end of every day. We refer to this time as "the golden hour" because this is when everything has a soft light and an amazing glow. The beginning and end are important ideas in the Bible too. In the book of Revelation, Jesus refers to Himself as "the alpha and omega—the beginning and the end." I've always understood this to mean that Jesus has always existed and will always exist.

But there's another meaning here that is pretty amazing.

Among Jewish rabbis, it's normal to use the first and last letters of the Hebrew alphabet to describe the entirety of something. So, when Jesus said He was the beginning and the end, He was identifying Himself as the God of the entire Bible! And while alpha and omega are the first and last letters of the Greek alphabet, Jesus was Jewish, and in Hebrew, the first and last letters are the *aleph* (א, pronounced "ah-lef") and the *tav* (ת, pronounced "tahv").

The Hebrew letters *aleph* and *tav* have specific meanings or images attributed to them. *Aleph* is represented by an ox and symbolizes strength and *tav* symbolizes truth or a signed contract.

So, when Jesus said He was the beginning and the end, He could also have been saying that He represented the strong covenant between us and God!

"I am the Alpha and the Omega, the Beginning and the End."
— Revelation 21:6

ישוע

SALVATION

YESHUA
SALVATION

Do you know what the name "Jesus" means?

For most of us, our name may not mean anything specific, but this is not the case with "Jesus."

You see, the name we translate in English as "Jesus" comes from the Hebrew word *Yeshua* (ישוע, pronounced "yeh-shoo-ah"), which literally means "to rescue" or "salvation." Jesus surely lives up to His name!

So, when Jesus invites Himself to the home of a tax collector named Zacchaeus, saying, "Today salvation has come to this house," it's possible He was using a pun—because "salvation" literally was in Zacchaeus's house that day!

Our salvation has a name. Our rescue has a name. As pastor Greg Laurie says, "Our hope has a name, and it's Jesus."

This is the name that causes the sun to rise, all creation to worship, and brings light into the darkness! It's the name that brings hope to the hopeless, heals the broken hearted, and is the only name that is worthy of praise.

And just like Jesus, your name means something too. Yes, it may identify you, and it may even define your credibility and reputation; but more importantly, your name is significant because God knows it. What's even more astonishing is that God has prepared for you a new name, a special name that He will give to those who are saved (Revelation 2:17).

So let me ask you two questions today:

Do you live with the confidence of knowing that the God who created the universe knows your name?

And, has "salvation" come to your house?

Jesus said to him, "Today salvation has come to this house, because this man, too, is a son of Abraham." — Luke 19:9

DAVAR
THE WORD

Has God's Word changed you?

Did you know that the word *Word* appears in the Old Testament more than 1,340 times?

The Hebrew word we translate as "word" is *davar* (דבר, pronounced "davar"), which in the verb form can also mean "command," "promise," and "act." This means that when we read the Word of God, we are not just reading text on a page—we're taking in God's promises and commandments.

And Numbers 23:19 reminds us that when God speaks a word, He acts on that word. When he makes a promise, He fulfills that promise. Whenever God says something, He follows through on that word.

Jesus, who is the Word of God, said that our words and actions carry much weight because they come from the overflow of our heart.

I love the way my friend Bob Goff says that "words people say not only have a shelf life, but have the ability to shape life" because it's an important reminder of the power our words can have.

So, the question is, how will your actions and the words you speak, text, email, and post to social media shape your life, and the lives of the people around you? Will your words and actions reflect the Word of God today and give glory back to Him?

See, we are called to do more than just read God's Word—we need to respond and act according to what we read. That's when God's Word doesn't just inform us; it transforms us.

Who's ready to be transformed by, and act upon, the Word of God today?

But don't just listen to God's word. You must do what it says. Otherwise, you are only fooling yourselves. — James 1:22 NLT

מים חיים

LIVING WATER

MAYIM CHAYYIM
LIVING WATER

Want a new perspective on the Bible?

In the first century, the people of Israel used to refer to any form of naturally flowing water—water that came directly from God—as *mayim chayyim* (מים חיים, pronounced "may-im khay-yim"), which means "living water." This water was quite literally a source of life for people who lived in the desert.

And, the first believers also referred to the Scriptures as *mayim chayyim*! They believed both water and the Torah came directly from God, and both were required for physical and spiritual health.

That's why reading Scripture should change the way you see the world and give you life!

What we read in the Bible should impact the way we act, the way we talk, the way we endure our problems, and the way we approach our relationships. But how often do we miss the Bible being a source of life because reading it feels like a chore?

Scripture becomes a source of life when you realize that following the guidance inside makes your life better and makes you better at life.

As author Christine Caine says when facing a tough season, "The best thing to do is pick up my Bible and remind myself of what God says."

Has God's Word changed your perspective of the world? If so, how?

"Whoever believes in me, as Scripture has said, rivers of living water will flow from within them." — John 7:38

רועה-צאן

SHEPHERD OF A FLOCK

RO'EH TZON
SHEPHERD OF A FLOCK

What is a "good shepherd"?

Jesus once described himself as a "good shepherd" who would lay down his life to protect his sheep—something I always understood in theory but missed the significance of because of where I grew up.

See, in most western countries, sheep are kept safe inside fenced-off fields with food and water—so they don't really need a shepherd.

But even today in Israel, there are very few fences, so sheep often wander through the desert where they can be attacked by any number of predators. This is where Jesus calls His followers—to be out in the world—where we *have* to rely on Jesus as our shepherd and have faith in His promises.

While the phrase "good shepherd" is not used in the Hebrew Bible, the Hebrew word we translate as "shepherd" is *ro'eh tzon* (רועה-צאן, pronounced "ro-eh tsone"), which is made up of two words. The first, *ro'eh*, means "herder," and the second, *tzon*, means "sheep."

The picture that the prophet Isaiah gives us of a *ro'eh tzon* is of someone who does more than just watches over sheep—the shepherd is a caring, loving companion. Isaiah says God is a like a shepherd who "will carry the lambs in his arms, holding them close to his heart." (Isaiah 40:11 NLT).

So, when Jesus says He is "the good shepherd," we should be reminded that no matter what situation we face, He will be with us, holding us close to His heart and lovingly caring for us.

Are you going through a rough season right now? If so, have confidence that Jesus is your good companion through it all. And He wants you to rely on Him for everything you need to get through this season.

Don't give up hope!

"I am the good shepherd; I know my own sheep, and they know me."
— John 10:14 NLT

RUACH HAKODESH
HOLY SPIRIT

Are you being transformed by God?

On the surf coast of Victoria, Australia, there are amazing, bent-over trees everywhere. The trees are bent over so far that the top leaves touch the ground!

But here's the thing: these trees are not deformed; they have actually been shaped this way.

You see, despite a strong trunk, deep roots, and thick branches, these trees have been shaped by the strong prevailing winds that blow through the region. The transformation process began the moment they were planted. These trees are strong and healthy, but they have been influenced by the power of the wind.

I think these trees are an awesome picture of the way the Spirit of God transforms us.

The Hebrew word we translate as wind is *ruach* (רוח, pronounced "roo'-akh"), which also means "Spirit" or "breath" of God. And when we choose to let the *ruach* of God transform and influence us, we will look different—just like these bent-over trees in Australia.

When we are transformed by God, we will stand out.

All of us are influenced and transformed by something—either the people we spend time with, the choices we make, or the *Ruach HaKodesh* of God.

We come to Christ as sinners drawn to his mercy. The Spirit reshapes us into saints—men and women who are holy before God. Choosing to follow Jesus transforms us.

You see, your life and faith don't get transformed by chance. They get transformed by choice.

Instead, let the Spirit renew your thoughts and attitudes.
— Ephesians 4:23 NLT

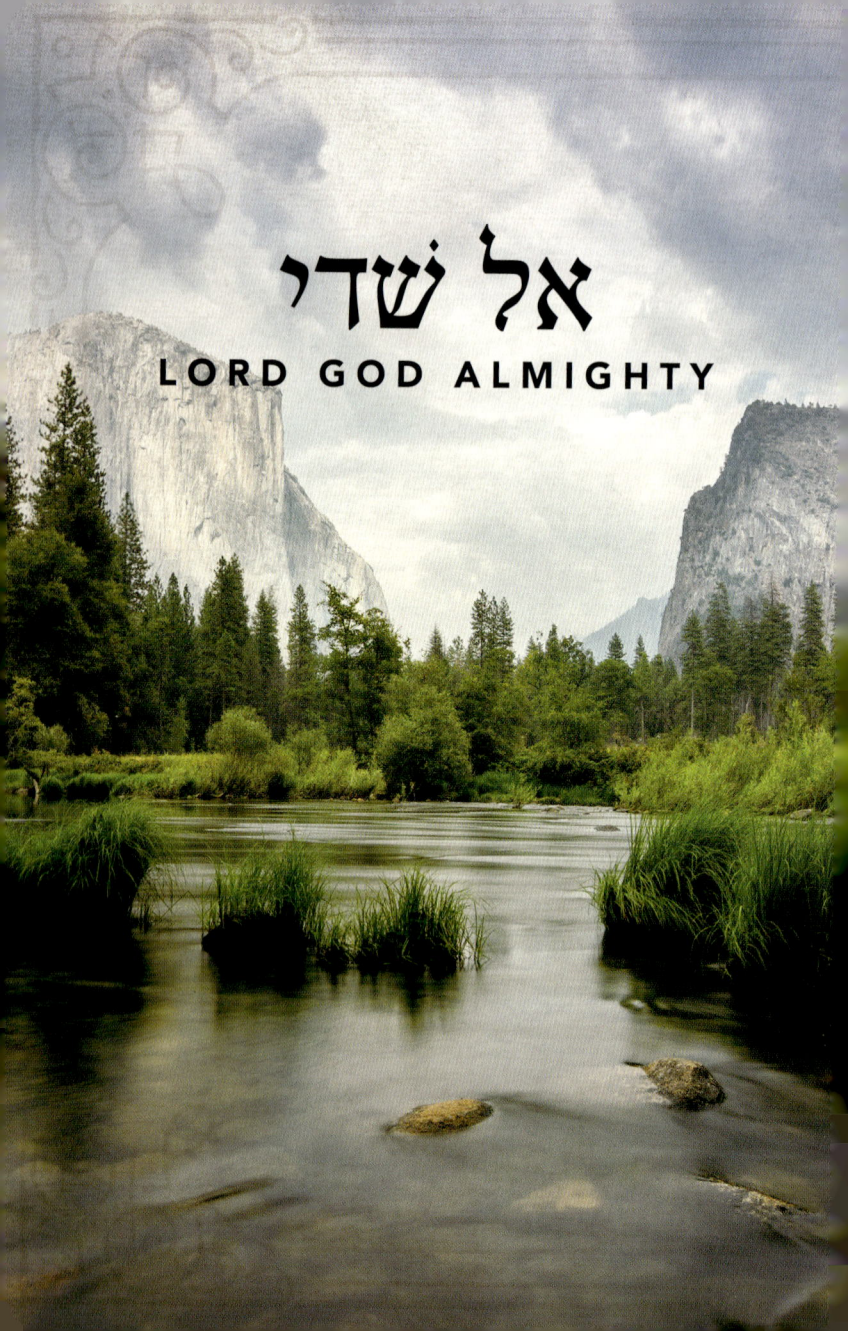

EL SHADDAI
LORD GOD ALMIGHTY

Need a miracle today?

We all face times in life when we are in what seems like an impossible situation, when we need God to show up and do something miraculous.

Maybe you are in one now as you read these words.

There's a story in the first book of the Bible where God makes what seems an impossible promise to a couple. He promises them that they will have children—despite the fact that they are both extremely old. In fact, it seems so impossible that the couple laughs it off!

But before God makes the promise, He tells them that "I am God Almighty." This name is a declaration that this couple need not worry about the outcome, because He is "Almighty" and capable of anything. He is reminding them that nothing is impossible for God!

In Hebrew, this name God gives Himself is *El Shaddai* (שדי אל, pronounced "el shad-dai"), which we translate as "Lord God Almighty," but can also mean "All Powerful" or "The All-Sufficient God." The idea behind this name is that not only is God a source of strength and power, but He is also able to meet all the needs of His people.

This means that no matter what you're going through today, God can be a firm foundation, source of hope, and strong tower because He is almighty and all-sufficient.

Are you in an impossible situation?

Are you in need of a miracle? Do you need God to show up in your circumstance as *El Shaddai*?

God wants to remind you today to depend entirely on Him.

Holy, holy, holy is the Lord God Almighty, who was, and is, and is to come. — Revelation 4:8

אל עליון

GOD MOST HIGH

EL ELYON
GOD MOST HIGH

Should you put God first?

Have you ever been in a plane and looked out the window to see the sunset and clouds from a new perspective? Whenever I do this, my mind quickly goes to God. Specifically, I think of one of my favorite names for God in the Bible, "God Most High."

In Hebrew, this name is *El Elyon* (אל עליון, pronounced "El el-Yohn"), which literally translates as "God Most High," but implies *so* much more than this.

It would be easy to assume that this name refers to God being above us in heaven, but the words *Most High* here actually refer to God being mightier, stronger, more holy, more powerful, and more worthy of worship than anything created. It implies that there is nothing that can be placed ahead of Him or over Him.

So, this name is actually a call to action for us.

It suggests that whenever we prioritize something ahead of God, we remove Him from the place in our lives that only He can occupy.

But let's be honest, it's easy to get distracted, right? Our jobs, kids, spouses, hobbies, work and sports can all become more important than our relationship with God.

But I've learned that if I want to have "life to the full" like Jesus promised, I have to prioritize my relationship with Him.

It's like Academy Award-winning actor Denzel Washington once said: "Put God first in everything you do. There has never been a time when God didn't direct, protect, or correct me."

For the LORD Most High is awesome, the great King over all the earth.
— Psalm 47:2

THE LORD OF HOSTS

YAHWEH SABAOTH
THE LORD OF HOSTS

Are you facing an uphill battle?

Sometimes life gets so difficult that we refer to the situation we are facing as a battle. These are times when things seem extremely complicated, stressful, and hard.

Whenever I'm facing an uphill battle, I find peace in knowing that one of the names for God found in the Bible is *Yahweh Sabaoth* (יהוה צבאות, pronounced "Yahweh tze-vah-oth").

This name is used more than 570 times in the Bible (depending on your translation) and means "Lord of Hosts," which refers specifically to God being the commander of the heavenly army.

The word *host* is an old term referring to an army, so this name defines God as the Lord or captain of the army in heaven, which may seem strange to us in the modern world.

But the point of this name for us today is that God fights for us. It means He protects and defends us. God is always in our corner!

And God being our *Yahweh Sabaoth* underlines what the Apostle Paul wrote to the Jesus followers in Rome, that "if God is for us, who can ever be against us?" (Romans 8:31 NLT).

So, no matter what you're facing today, no matter how hard the battle ahead, and no matter how overwhelming the situation may seem, you have the Lord of Hosts in your corner ready to fight on your behalf!

That should give *all* of us hope!

The LORD will fight for you; you need only to be still. — Exodus 14:14

EL HAKKAVOD
THE GOD OF GLORY

Do you minimize God's glory?

When we don't understand what God's glory is, we risk missing the application of God's glory in our own situation. This means you won't be able to live *for* God's glory until you understand life *with* God's glory.

You see, Christians on Instagram will speak of God's glory when they post a sunset image like this because we translate the word *glory* as "splendor" or "beauty"—but God's glory is so much more than that!

The Hebrew word we translate as "glory" in the Bible is *kabod* (כבוד, pronounced "Kah-vode"), which means "heavy" or "weighty." *Kabod* is also the root of a word meaning "rich" in Hebrew. In Bible times, they would say a rich man was "heavy with wealth," in the same way we might say a rich person is "loaded" today.

This word is also one of God's names, "The God of Glory," which in Hebrew is *El Hakkavod* (אל הכבוד, pronounced "el ha-kah-vode").

The idea behind this word and this name is that when we experience God's glory, we're experiencing the weight of His goodness, the weight of His beauty, and the weight of His mercy.

And because we misunderstand the meaning of the word, we miss the weight of God's compassion, mercy, and peace during hard times, instead becoming too focused on the fear and worry of our situation. This is why we need to remember that, as *Jesus Calling* author Sarah Young writes, "God's glory can reach you in the present—no matter how dark your circumstances may appear."

It's when life is hard, dark, and difficult that we need to experience the glory and full weight—*kabod*—of God's compassion.

Do you need to experience God's glory today?

The heavens declare the glory of God; the skies proclaim the work of his hands. — Psalm 19:1

ᲧAHWEH TSIDKENU
THE LORD IS OUR RIGHTEOUSNESS

What is *righteousness*?

We read in the Bible that the righteous will be "remembered forever" (Psalm 112:6) and that God loves people who "pursue righteousness" (Proverbs 15:9). But I think this is my favorite verse about being righteous: "The path of the righteous is like the light of dawn, which shines brighter and brighter until full day" (Proverbs 4:18 ESV). I think we all want a life that continues to shine brighter the longer we live, right?

Well, the answer is found in that word—*righteousness*.

I used to think *righteousness* meant knowing a lot of Bible verses and not doing things that were against God—to have right standing.

The Hebrew word we translate as righteousness is *tsedaqah* (צדקה, pronounced "tsed-ah-kah"), which means to help someone in need. *Tsedaqah* is about showing concern for the poor through charity and generosity. It's about serving the least, the last, and the lost. This is how we have a life that continues to shine brighter like the dawn—by serving people in need around us.

In this way, we are simply following the model Jesus set for us. After all, in prophesying about the coming Messiah, Jeremiah said that "this will be his name: 'The LORD Is Our Righteousness'" (Jeremiah 23:6). This name in Hebrew is *Yahweh Tsidkenu* (יהוה צידקנו, pronounced "Yah-weh Tsid-kay-new").

Can you imagine what the world would be like if every follower of Jesus were known for their compassion and generosity? Imagine what your own community would be like if every follower of Jesus pursued opportunities to help people in need!

So, how will you pursue righteousness—that is, pursue opportunities to serve people in need and be generous—today?

Blessed are those who hunger and thirst for righteousness, for they shall be satisfied. — Matthew 5:6 ESV

EL GIBBOR
THE MIGHTY GOD

Who is your biggest hero?

When I was growing up, my heroes were either athletes or musicians.

These are the people I aspired to be like, and I always thought it would be awesome to be friends with someone whom other people admired.

But this all changed when I started taking seriously my decision to follow Jesus. That's when a rabbi friend told me that one of the names for God in the Hebrew Bible is *El Gibbor* (אל גבור, pronounced "El gib-bore").

This title, *El Gibbor*, is made up of two Hebrew words. The first is *El*, which is the singular form of *Elohim*, the name of the one true God. The second word is *Gibbor* (גבור, pronounced "gib-bore"), which translates as "mighty," "strong," or "hero."

The idea of *El Gibbor* is that in a world where we often define our heroes by their athletic ability, their popularity, their skill or talent in a given field, the size of their bank account, their business savvy, or the number of social media followers they have, only God is truly worthy of the title. Only God is *El Gibbor*.

And here's the great thing for followers of Jesus: the prophet Isaiah wrote that the Messiah would be known as *El Gibbor*, the "Mighty God" (Isaiah 9:6). This means our rabbi is also our hero!

No matter what sort of hero you need today—one who saves, who protects, or who inspires—you have that in Jesus.

For the LORD your God is living among you. He is a mighty savior.
— Zephaniah 3:17 NLT

עתיק יומין
ANCIENT OF DAYS

ATIK YOMIN
ANCIENT OF DAYS

What will God do tomorrow?

Do you ever wonder what God has planned for your future? There are times in all of our lives when it can feel like we're walking in a fog and can only see a few feet in front of us, where the next step seems unclear and the future uncertain.

Wouldn't life be easier if we just knew what God had planned for our future and how He had used our past to prepare us for what is to come?

This is why one of my favorite names for God in the Bible is *Atik Yomin* (עתיק יומין, pronounced "ah-teek yoh-meen"), which means "Ancient of Days" and is found only in chapter 7 of the book of Daniel. Daniel was originally written in Aramaic, so this is not a "Hebrew name," but it was a name by which God revealed himself to the Hebrew people.

Daniel uses this name when he has a vision of God on His throne in heaven. The idea behind the name is that God is eternal and exists outside the boundaries of time. This means He existed *before* the existence of days! God had no beginning and He will have no end.

This also means that God, as *Atik Yomin*, always has been and always will be watching over your life.

You might be in a fog and uncertain about your future or the next step you should take, but the Ancient of Days is never uncertain. He knows the beginning from the end, which means that all of us as His children can have hope and confidence knowing that He has the past, the present, and the future under his control.

Are you worried about your future? Are you desperate to see what your next step should be?

If so, take a moment to focus on God, remind yourself of a time He came through for you in the past, and step confidently into the future knowing that the Ancient of Days is watching over you.

As I looked, thrones were set in place, and the Ancient of Days took his seat. — Daniel 7:9 NIV

YAHWEH
LORD

Do you know what word "Yahweh" appears 6,200 times in the Bible?

If a word appears that many times in Scripture, it has to be important. Well, that word is a name. It's *Yahweh* (יהוה, pronounced "Yah-weh"), the personal name of God.

You may see this word written as YHWH (no vowels) or as Jehovah (English transliteration) in some Bibles, but in Hebrew this word means "He will be." We learn this word when Moses asks God his name, and God responds with "I Am Who I Am," which essentially means that God does not change—He simply *is*.

Over the centuries, Jewish believers wanted to honor this divine name so much that they replaced it in Scripture with the Hebrew word for "LORD," which is *adonai*, because *Yahweh* was too sacred to say out loud. The English translators of the Bible continued this idea, which is why your Bible has the word LORD in all caps—the word that serves as a replacement for the personal name of God.

So, why is any of this important?

Well, whether your translation of the Bible renders it as "Yahweh," "YHWH," "Jehovah," or "LORD," this is the divine, personal name of God—and He wants *you* to know His name!

This is significant because the biblical poet David wrote that people who know God's name will trust Him (Psalm 9:10), and I want you to trust God.

Author and speaker Nick Vujicic once said, "Hope is in the name of God," because when you know God, you know His "immeasurable love and grace." Understanding God's name allows you to relate to Him on a new level, beyond just His title as Lord. As author John Mark Comer writes, God is "a relational being who wants to know and be known" by His people.

God is known by many names, but His personal name is יהוה—*Yahweh*.

Do *you* know God by this name?

Those who know your name trust in you because you have not abandoned those who seek you, LORD. — Psalm 9:10 CSB

אל עולם

THE EVERLASTING GOD

EL OLAM
THE EVERLASTING GOD

Need hope today?

If you need hope to get through your current situation—or to get through life in general—this may be the most important thing you read today.

There is a Hebrew name for God that I love, *El Olam* (עולם אל, pronounced "El oh-lam"), which we translate in our English Bibles as "Eternal God" or "Everlasting God." Abraham gives God this name when he is standing in the land God promised to him and he plants a single tamarisk tree to declare the faithfulness of God.

The name *El Olam* is later picked up by several other biblical authors including Malachi, who says this name means God's promises are reliable, and Isaiah, who writes that you can always find hope and strength in a God that never stops loving you.

And that is why I love this name for God—because it's a reminder for us that God is faithful and will always come through for those who follow him.

In my darkest moments, when I feel alone, weak, discouraged, lost, and without hope, I am encouraged to know that the Everlasting God is with me, He won't grow tired, and He promises to give me life to the full—no matter what I'm facing.

It may not happen in the time frame you want it to happen, but *El Olam*, the Eternal God, will not fail to come through on His plans and promises for you. This name not only gives me hope and peace—it also gives me a purpose.

You see, if God is working for me at all times, then I don't need to waste time worrying. I can find purpose in my situation knowing that God already has the outcome sorted.

When it comes to your life, you can't count the days that remain, but you can make the days that remain count.

And you make them count by trusting that God is in control and that He is reliable.

Are you ready to make every day count?

Do you not know? Have you not heard? The LORD is the everlasting God, the Creator of the ends of the earth. — Isaiah 40:28

יהוה רפא

THE LORD HEALS

YAHWEH ROPHE
THE LORD HEALS

Does your past impact your present?

If you have a past you would prefer to forget, I understand completely. You see, I come from a difficult childhood that includes years of sexual abuse—but I refuse to let that imprison me.

That's because my favorite Bible verse comes from the Apostle Paul, who wrote that when we choose to follow Jesus, we leave our past behind and we become "new creations." This verse means so much to me that I have it tattooed down the length of my arm as a permanent reminder that my past no longer affects my future.

The old has gone—the new has come.

And this is why God is called *Yahweh Rophe* (יהוה רפא, pronounced "Yah-weh row-phe"), "The God Who Heals." You see, we often think of God's healing coming to us only when we're sick or injured, but the authors of the Bible remind us that God also heals emotional wounds, mental suffering, physical and spiritual fatigue, and stress and anxiety.

This is why I'm passionate about helping people who have survived backgrounds like mine, because I believe you cannot grab hold of your future if you keep holding on to your past. While we may be products of our past, we don't have to be prisoners of it—not if we follow the God who heals.

Musician LeCrae says, "Peace doesn't mean you won't have problems, it means problems won't have you." So if there's a piece of your past that you want to make peace with today, I encourage you to pray about it.

Pray specifically that any open wounds from your past will become scars, because when wounded people see our scars, they know there is a healer—and His name is *Yahweh Rophe*!

Anyone who belongs to Christ has become a new person. The old life is gone; a new life has begun! — 2 Corinthians 5:17 NLT

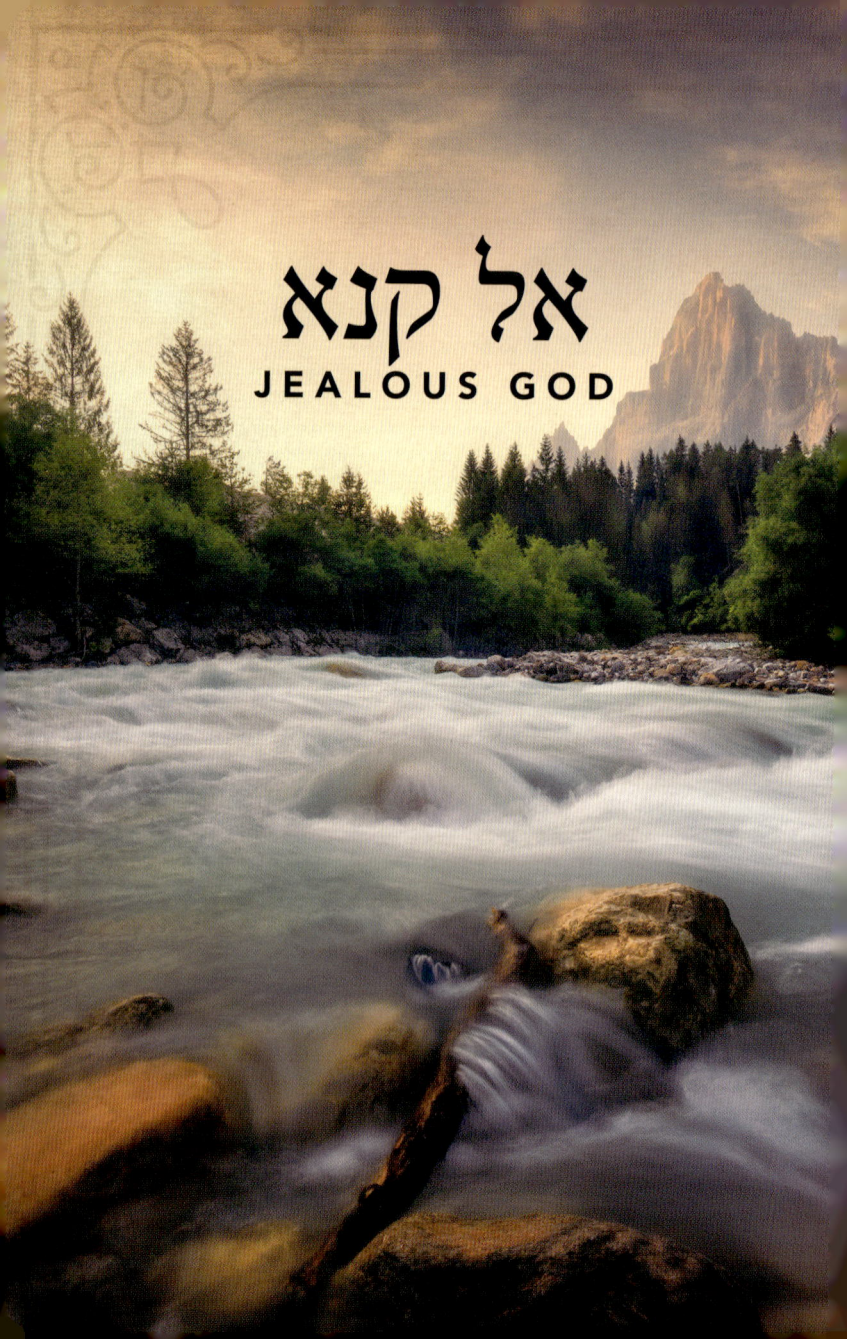

EL KANNAH
JEALOUS GOD

Are you too distracted for God?

We are constantly surrounded by things vying for our attention—from family and friends to social media, advertising, streaming services, and TV. There is so much noise in the world that it can be hard to focus on the things that truly matter.

If we're honest with ourselves, this often includes God. We get so distracted that we push God aside and push Him down our list of priorities.

But Scripture describes God as *El Kannah* (אל קנא, pronounced "el kannah"), which means "The Jealous God."

Now, in modern English, jealousy is a negative emotion that is often defined as "envy," but God's jealousy is rooted in His love for you and in His insistence that He will not share his position as your top priority.

This is why Jesus said to love God "with all your heart and with all your soul and with all your strength and with all your mind" (Luke 10:27).

God is jealous for all of you! He wants every inch of your soul, every thought of your mind, everything you desire and feel! He wants your whole attention because of the great love He has for you!

This is why the first of the Ten Commandments prohibits the worship of anything other than God.

And while most of us would agree with the idea that God wants our whole attention, in practice we often fall short. We want to spend eternity with God, but it's as if we often don't want to spend too much time with Him *now*.

With all the distractions around us pulling us in every direction except toward God, we need to do whatever we can to prioritize time with Him.

So, how are you putting God first today and every day?

Do not worship any other god, for the LORD, whose name is Jealous, is a jealous God. — Exodus 34:14

אש אכלה

CONSUMING FIRE

ESH OKELAH
CONSUMING FIRE

How should Christians act in a polarized world?

As a follower of Jesus, how are you supposed to act in a world that has become so divisive and hostile? When a polarizing political or social issue arises and things get heated in a conversation or on social media, how should you respond to the person who mocks or insults you?

The author of Proverbs says to "heap burning coals" on the head of your enemy (Proverbs 25:22), which sometimes sounds like a great idea. However, in the previous verse we are told to do this by giving our enemy food and something to drink! How can we show such mercy toward those who have wronged us?

Well, in the study of written texts, there is an interpretive technique called the "Law of First Mention" which suggests that often the context in which a word first appears in a text establishes its fundamental meaning. In Genesis 15, the idea of burning coals is first mentioned when God appears to Abraham as a "smoking firepot" filled with burning coals that cause smoke to come from the spout.

If the Law of First Mention was applied here, it would mean that fire and smoke would represent God throughout the Bible. We see examples of this in the burning bush and in the pillar of fire and smoke that led the Israelites through the desert. And one of the Hebrew names for God is *Esh Okelah* (אש אכלה, pronounced "Esh O-khe-lah"), which means "Consuming Fire."

If God is a Consuming Fire, he will ultimately deal with all unrighteousness. We do not need to seek revenge or vindication. We can trust that even as we show mercy and kindness to our enemies, God's perfect justice will prevail. Instead of heaping "burning coals," we might lead our enemies to encounter God as a Consuming Fire.

As followers of Jesus, we can pray that the people who have hurt or wronged us will experience God's perfect justice *and* His mercy in Christ.

Has someone hurt you? Pray that God will reveal himself to that person and that He will consume all injustice and wrongdoing. Pray for God's mercy to prevail.

The Temple was filled with smoke from God's glory and power.
— Revelation 15:8 NLT

יהוה יראה

THE LORD WILL PROVIDE

ΥΛΗWΕΗ JIRΕΗ
THE LORD WILL PROVIDE

Do you *really* trust God?

How would you feel if your friends and neighbors could easily tell how much you trust God?

Well, in the days of the Bible, your neighbors could know how much faith you had simply by looking over your fence to see the size of your corners!

In the book of Leviticus, God told His people to leave the corners of their fields uncut at harvest so the poor could pick the leftover grain and have food to eat. This was called "gleaning," which in Hebrew is *leket* (לקט, pronounced "leh-ket") and refers to this biblical law of being generous to the poor at harvest time.

People who trusted that God would provide enough for them could be generous, so they had big corners on their land. But people who didn't trust that God would provide enough for them had small corners, thus leaving less for people in need.

Having big corners meant you trusted God to provide for you. It meant you trusted in *Yahweh Jireh*, which is the Hebrew name for God, meaning "The Lord Will Provide" (יהוה יראה, pronounced "Yahweh yeer-eh").

But if you were worried about God coming through for you, then you probably had small corners because you were trying to cover your bases. As pastor Craig Groeschel says, "The things we worry about the most are the hints we trust God with the least." So, small corners meant you were worried about God's ability to provide for your future.

Which leads to an important question: If we could look over *your* "fence," what would we see?

Do you trust that *Yahweh Jireh* will provide for you?

How big will your corners be today?

When you harvest the crops of your land, do not harvest the grain along the edges of your fields...Leave it for the poor and the foreigners living among you. — Leviticus 23:22

QEDOSH YISRA'EL
HOLY ONE OF ISRAEL

What does God's name mean?

There's a name in the Bible that is used for God that I'm sure is a name most of us skim over as we read, but taking a closer look at it could be the thing you need most right now.

The name is "Holy One of Israel," which in Hebrew is Qedosh Yisra'el (ישראל קדוש, pronounced "ke-dosh yis-ra-ail").

The first word, *Qedosh*, means "Holy One" and refers directly to God's nature. God is holy.

Holiness is typically translated in English to mean "separated," "transcendent," or "exalted," because God is perfect. While this correctly implies that he is totally worthy of our devotion, it can also make God seem far off and distant. But that's not how God defines Himself.

You see, when God told the prophet Isaiah to tell the Israelites He was specifically their "Holy One," He was letting his people know He was with them and for them.

And the implication of this for you today is that God is the Holy One of *you*, just as He is the Holy One of me. This means God is with you and for you, and He is with me and for me.

He is with you in your pain and challenging circumstance. He is for you when everything seems to be falling apart. When life gets hard and chaos seems to be surrounding you, God promises to be present.

This God who is perfect and holy hears your cries because He is the Holy One of *all* His people.

"For I am the LORD, your God, the Holy One of Israel, your Savior."
— Isaiah 43:3 NLT

שכינה

THE PRESENCE OF GOD

SHEKINAH
THE PRESENCE OF GOD

When have you felt closest to God?

For me, it was the day I spend in the Negev Desert of Israel with my youngest daughter, Jordyn.

We were in the Negev, a place the Israelites walked through during their desert wandering in the biblical story of the Exodus, as the sun was setting. We were there with some other friends, all of whom were either photographing the sunset and the local shepherds nearby, flying drones, or video chatting with loved ones to share the experience.

It was in the community, the creativity, the laughter, and the desert surroundings that I felt the presence of God.

In Hebrew, the presence of God is called the *Shekinah* (שכינה, pronounced "She-chi-nah"). While this word is not found in the Hebrew Bible, it is used by rabbis as a way of describing the presence of God in the Bible.

When Christians hear the word *Shekinah*, we typically think of the pillar of fire and smoke that went ahead of the Israelites in the story of the Exodus—but the word means so much more than that. *Shekinah* is the name for the presence of God manifested in the world.

First-century believers would experience this presence in several ways: the beauty of a sunrise or sunset, enjoying a deep encounter with a friend or relative, or even studying Scripture with others.

I know God was present with my daughter and me in the desert that day because His *Shekinah* was obvious. It was exactly like author Max Lucado says: "God's present is his presence. His greatest gift is himself."

So, when was the last time you experienced God's presence? Was it at the ocean? During a hike in the mountains? In a small-group Bible study? Knowing when you experience God can help you know how to experience God the next time you need to know He is with you.

But as for me, how good it is to be near God! I have made the Sovereign LORD my shelter, and I will tell everyone about the wonderful things you do. — Psalm 73:28 NLT

יהוה צורי

THE LORD MY ROCK

YAHWEH TSURI
THE LORD MY ROCK

What is spiritual maturity?

People often ask me what books, podcasts, or Bible studies I recommend to help them become more "spiritually mature," but what does that even mean? James describes spiritual maturity as being doers of the Word and not hearers only (James 1:22). Paul describes it as becoming more and more like Christ (Ephesians 4:13).

Author Lisa Bevere says spiritual maturity is when you "run to God as a first response, not a last resort." Most importantly, we become spiritually mature when we take Jesus at his Word and live in obedience to Him.

It's like this fern I photographed in Tennessee—it gets everything it needs to survive by attaching itself to the rock. Likewise, our spiritual maturity comes from being connected to *The* Rock.

The Hebrew word translated as "rock" in the Bible is *tsuri*, which refers to stability and security. This is why one of the names of God is "The Lord My Rock" (יהוה צורי, pronounced "Yah-weh tsu-ree"), because in God we find security. And spiritual maturity is about having the security that Jesus is who He claimed to be.

That's why, when people ask me what they should read for spiritual growth, I always suggest a monthly reading of the four books written about Jesus' life! I know that reading Matthew, Mark, Luke, and John every month is a lot, but that's the most practical way I know to learn about what Jesus said and did so you can follow His example.*

So, how are you becoming more spiritually mature? In other words, how are you becoming more like Jesus?

The LORD is my rock. — Psalm 18:2

*To make this easier, I wrote a reading plan for the YouVersion Bible app called "Follow the Rabbi," which walks you through all four Gospels in a month and includes devotionals to help you get the most out of what you read. Just search for my name in the app.

YAHWEH SHAMMAH
THE LORD IS THERE

Have you ever wondered where God was?

Maybe you have faced a difficult situation, or experienced a great loss, or simply had a prayer that seemed unanswered, and so you asked yourself if God was even aware of your circumstance.

I know I have!

It's in these times that I remind myself of the Hebrew name for God, *Yahweh Shammah* (יהוה שמה, pronounced "shawm-maw"), which means "The Lord Is There."

God revealed this name for Himself when he gave the prophet Ezekiel a vision of a fully restored Jerusalem and said that He would be there in that place. The point was for God's people, who were in exile at the time, to find hope in knowing that even when all seemed lost, they could count on God being present with them.

And the same is true for us today.

In fact, Jesus told us that He would always be there for all of his followers. He echoed the name *Yahweh Shammah* when He said, "I am with you always, even to the end of the age" (Matthew 28:20 NLT).

The idea behind this promise, and the name *Yahweh Shammah*, is that as His child, you were designed to both enjoy the presence of God and reflect the presence of God to the world.

So, wherever you are, no matter what your circumstances or your need, no matter how lost everything seems, you can be sure that God is there with you because He is *Yahweh Shammah*.

"Teach these new disciples to obey all the commands I have given you. And be sure of this: I am with you always, even to the end of the age."
— Matthew 28:20 NLT

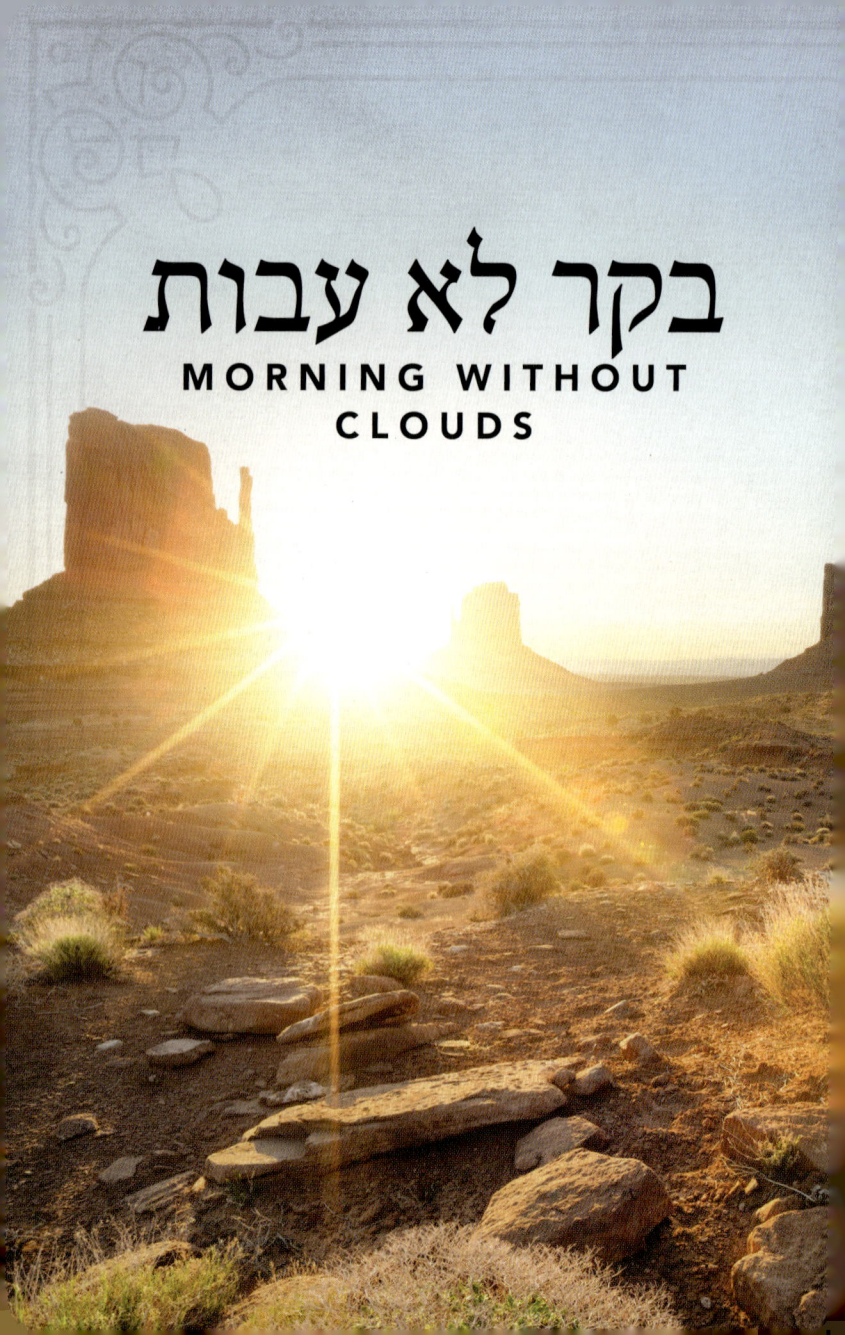

BOKER LO AVOT
MORNING WITHOUT CLOUDS

Can I share with you the coolest name for Jesus?

Whenever I get to photograph a sunrise when there are barely any clouds in the sky, I'm reminded of one of the Hebrew names for the Messiah—"Morning Without Clouds." Now, this name may seem a bit odd, but let me explain.

This phrase comes from 2 Samuel 23:4, which says the Messiah will be "like the light of morning at sunrise on a cloudless morning." The Hebrew phrase we translate as "Morning Without Clouds" is *boker lo avot* (בקר לא עבות, pronounced "bo-ker low ah-vot"), and the idea behind this name is that the kingdom of the Messiah will light up the world instantly, like a sunrise when there are no clouds in the sky to block or diffuse the light.

Now, as a photographer, I prefer cloudy sunrises, because the shadows and contrast the clouds create in the sky usually make for a more dramatic picture. Clouds in the sky also cause the morning light to increase more gradually, so the golden hour is naturally extended. But when I first started following Jesus, I didn't move gradually from darkness to light—it happened in the blink of an eye.

It was like a quote I read from pastor Rick Warren: "Living in the light of eternity changes your priorities." My priorities changed instantly, which is why I believe that following Jesus makes your life better and makes you better at life.

If you follow Jesus, then you represent the Morning Without Clouds.

And this means you should always bring light into your world—whether that's in your family, a business deal, a relationship, or your neighborhood. You should bring light, peace, and hope to every situation.

And now more than ever, the world needs light, peace, and hope.

How will your words and actions today shine brightly like a morning without clouds?

He dawns on them like the morning light, like the sun shining forth on a cloudless morning. — 2 Samuel 23:4 ESV

ΥΛHWEh MΛGEN
GOD IS MY SHIELD

What does it mean that God is your "shield"?

Christians often say this when their world is being shaken—but seriously, what does this term mean to you?

The Hebrew phrase we translate as "God Is My Shield" is *Yahweh Magen* (יהוה מגן, pronounced "Yah-weh mah-gane"). This phrase means "protect." The idea is that when we are weary from stress and anxiety, and when we're depleted from fear, God protects us.

This is one of God's titles in the Scriptures, and He first gives it to Himself when he speaks with Abram, saying, "Do not be afraid, Abram, I am your shield" (Genesis 15:1).

The idea of this title for Abram and for us is that God is a barrier of protection in whom we can find rest and hope.

Let's be honest: in some way, we're all facing a world that is being shaken right now. And my prayer is that when times are tough, you would head straight toward your Shield for protection, rest, and hope.

And even if you feel you're being protected by God right now, there will be other times when you're facing a difficult situation and you won't necessarily sense His protection.

It's then that we need to remember the words of pastor Louie Giglio, who said, "God leads us. He protects us. He guides us and cleans us and watches over us. He isn't a distant God."

If you're feeling shaken, fearful, or anxious today, then I pray you would find strength, hope, and encouragement from knowing that God is *your* shield.

But you, LORD, are a shield around me, my glory, the One who lifts my head high. — Psalm 3:3

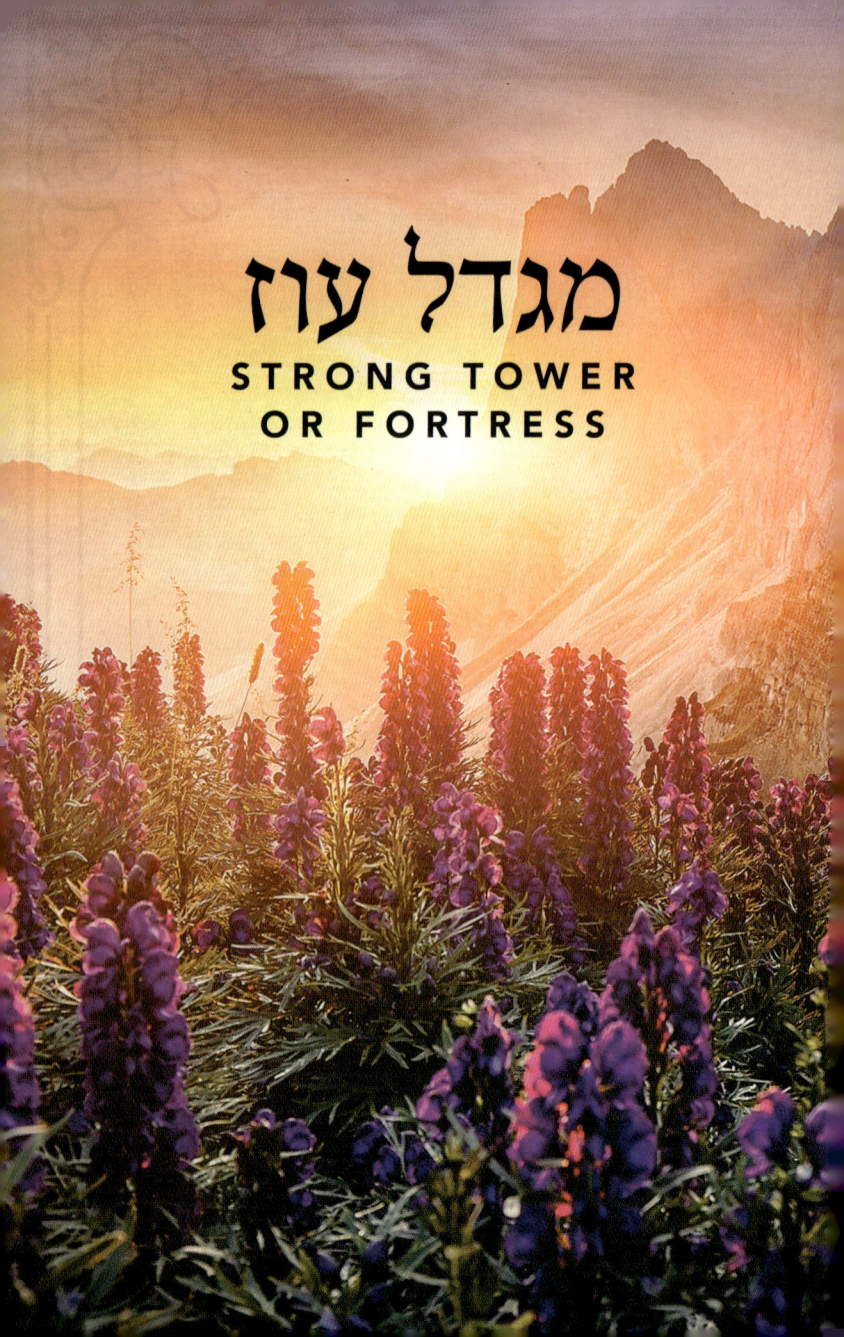

MIGDAL-OZ
STRONG TOWER
OR FORTRESS

Do you need some hope today?

Are you facing a tough situation and need a reminder that God is *for* you?

One of God's names in the Bible is *Migdal-Oz* (מגדל עוז, pronounced "mig-dawl ohze"), which means "Strong Tower" or "Fortress." The idea is that God is the foundation of a believer's life. There is a physical representation of this name in Israel called Masada—a 1,300-foot-high mountain in the desert of Judea.

And at least since Herod the Great, the mountain of Masada has been a tangible symbol of God's strength. It's possible that David fled to the same mountain when he was being pursued by King Saul. David compared the mountain to "a fortress" or "Masada." It was on the mountain, a natural fortress, that he took refuge. To David, this rock was a picture of God, and it inspired him to write, "The LORD is my rock, my fortress, and my savior; my God is my rock, in whom I find protection" (Psalm 18:2 NLT).

To David, this mountain represented God because it was a physical place where he found refuge and protection in a time of desperate spiritual and emotional need.

I wonder how many people need a tangible reminder that God is *their* strong tower, *their* refuge, and *their* safe place today.

If you need God to be your strong tower, your foundation, your safe place today, then I pray this image will bring you hope.

The LORD is my rock, my fortress, and my savior; my God is my rock, in whom I find protection. He is my shield, the power that saves me, and my place of safety. — Psalm 18:2 NLT

מלך

KING

MELEK
KING

What will heaven be like?

People often ask me what the Jewish scriptures say about heaven or what rabbis teach about where we go when we die.

Before I was a follower of Jesus, a tropical island surrounded by white sand, in the middle of a stunning ocean, was my idea of heaven. And I'm pretty sure most Christians think heaven is a place in the sky. But when Jesus talked about the kingdom of God or the kingdom of heaven (they are both the same), He painted a different picture.

He called heaven a kingdom because He defined God as the King—not just of Israel, but of every nation on earth. In Hebrew, "King" is *Melek* (מלך, pronounced "meh'-lek").

And the Hebrew phrase we translate as "the kingdom of heaven" is *Malkhut Shamayim* (מלכות שמים, pronounced "mal-koot sham-ay-im"), which doesn't just refer to a place, but also to people who submit to God's authority. This is why Jesus said that "the Kingdom of God is already among you," because *Malkhut Shamayim*—the kingdom of heaven—is wherever a person is living under the authority of God's word.

That means if you follow Jesus and submit to His authority, then you are already a citizen of the kingdom of heaven!

You see, God's kingdom is not just in the sky—it's anywhere that He is recognized as King. So, when we submit ourselves to God, we represent His kingdom on earth. When we serve people in need, when we act justly, when we apply mercy and compassion, or when we walk humbly, we act as citizens of God's kingdom.

The kingdom of heaven is not just a place we go to when we die. As pastor John Bevere says, "We are to succeed in this life by the standards of Heaven, not of our culture." That's because we live under the rule of Christ our King even while we wait for God's kingdom to come to earth fully.

I believe our role as followers of God is not just to bring people to heaven but to help people see the beauty of God's kingdom by how we live on earth. Are you living as a citizen of God's kingdom even now?

For the Kingdom of God is already among you. — Luke 17:21 NLT

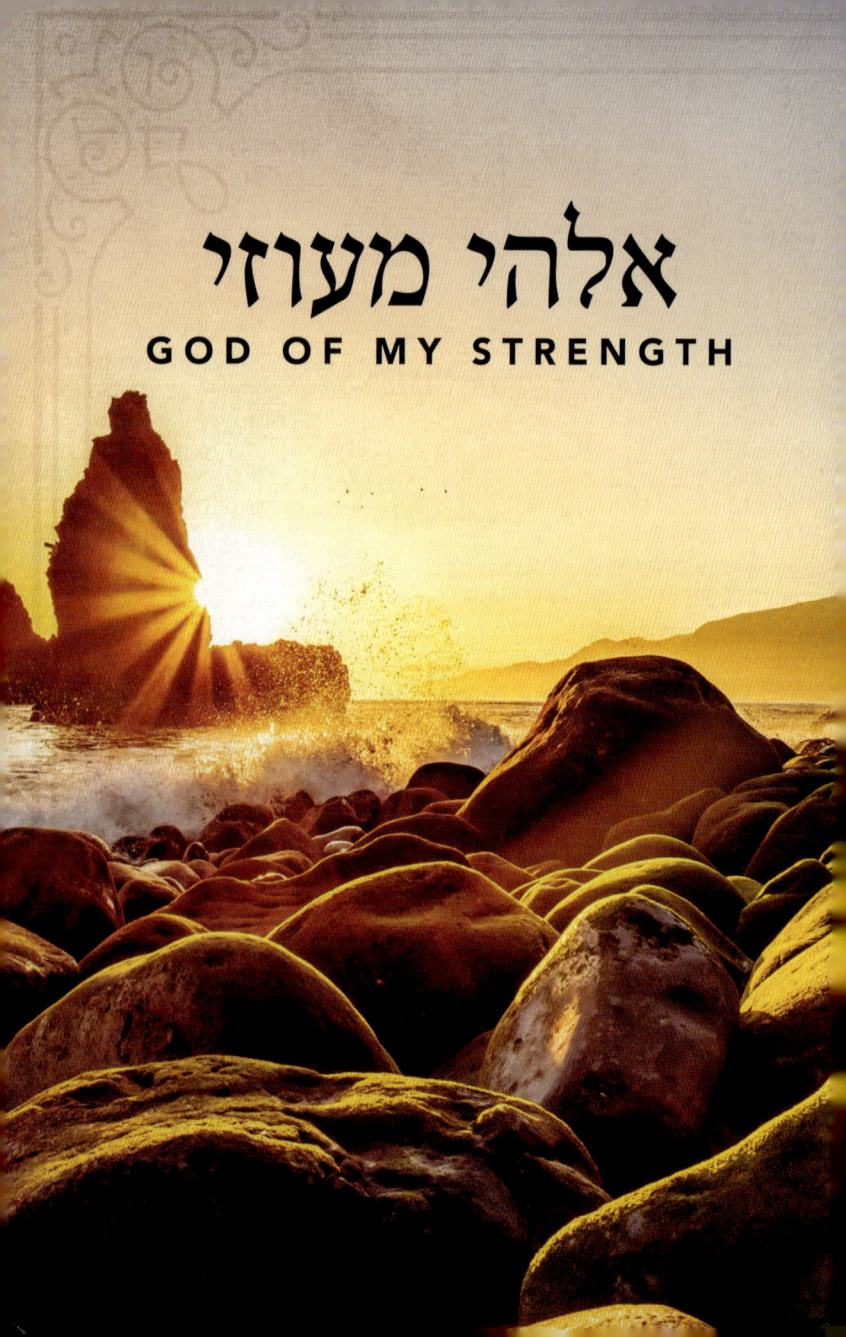

אלהי מעוזי

GOD OF MY STRENGTH

ELOHEI MA'UZZI
GOD OF MY STRENGTH

Is life complicated today?

Does it feel like life is taking its toll on you right now? There are times when we all get worn down by situations, weakened by circumstances, and stressed by daily struggles.

It's in these times that we need to remember that one of the names Moses gave God in the Bible is "God of My Strength."

In Hebrew, this name is *Elohei Ma'uzzi* (אלהי מעוזי, pronounced "el-oh-hey mah-uzi"), which also means "God My Stronghold" or "God Is My Fortress."

This is also the name David used after God steered him to victory over his enemies.

During times when life was chaotic and challenging, Moses and David turned to God to protect them from the outside world and give them strength they didn't naturally have.

Perhaps this is what you need today too.

If your life seems out of control, complicated, challenging, or chaotic, then let God be your strength today.

When you're completely overwhelmed by your situation, ask God to give you the strength to persevere.

And instead of trying to manufacture strength and courage on your own, allow God to protect you and give you a safe place to rest.

**The LORD is my strength and my defense; he has become my salvation.
— Exodus 15:2**

EL ECHAD
THE ONE GOD

Do you know your God-given purpose?

Well, if you want to discover your God-given purpose, all you need to do is remember the Hebrew word for the number *one*.

Let me explain.

You see, numbers mean a lot in the Hebrew language. The Hebrew word we translate as "one" is *echad* (אחד, pronounced "ekh-ahd"), which means so much more than just the number one.

Yes, *echad* means "one," but it can also be a compound "one," like one bunch of grapes has many grapes or one vine of tomatoes has multiple tomatoes. It also means "sameness" or "uniqueness," and, importantly, it also denotes unity of purpose. This is what Jesus meant when He said He and the Father were one—that together They have a unity of identity and of purpose.

And this purpose reflects the nature of the Hebrew name for God, *El Echad*, which means "The One God."

Jesus also explained that His followers would have that same unity of purpose, because just as He was one with His heavenly Father, we are one with Him (John 14:20). And what is that purpose? Well, it's simple—love God and love others.

Jesus didn't say our purpose was to follow religious rituals or to attend church a certain number of times each year. He didn't say our purpose was to exclude certain people. He didn't say it was about voting for a certain party or about nationalism. Jesus said our sole purpose was to love God and love the people around us.

But we betray what it means to follow Jesus when we let anything else get in the way of this purpose.

What will you do today to love God and love people?

"I and the Father are one." — John 10:30

יָצָר

THE CREATOR

YATSAR
THE CREATOR

Do you know how God sees you?

One of my favorite things to do is photograph a sunrise or sunset. I love to watch and photograph the amazing colors in the sky at these times of day.

But have you ever considered that God, your Creator, looks at you in the same way we look at a sunrise?

When God looks at you, He sees the beauty He created. He sees his "workmanship" (Ephesians 2:10 ESV).

The Bible says that God is your Creator, which in Hebrew is *Yatsar* (יצר, pronounced "yah-tsar").

When *Yatsar* looks at you, He sees a person who has been "wonderfully made" (Psalm 139:14). And it's cool that the Hebrew word we translate as "wonderfully" in this verse is *palah* (פלה, pronounced "pah-lah"), which means "distinct." You see, God says that from all the other people in the world, you are distinguishable to Him!

Today, I believe your Creator wants you to see yourself in the same way He sees you. I believe He wants you to know that He recognizes you and that you are loved and valued, even when

- you wake up feeling like you've failed or let Him down;
- you're worried that you don't live up to expectations;
- you're struggling to get out of bed;
- you feel stressed or worried;
- you're anxious and afraid.

Every day, God looks at you with the same delight we have when we see a stunning sunrise or sunset, so stop comparing your life to someone else's. As author Lisa Bevere says, "God made you uniquely. Don't ever trade that for the compromise of comparison."

Remember: you are God's child (John 1:12), you are free (Galatians 5:1), you are accepted (Romans 15:7), you are chosen (1 Thessalonians 1:4), and you are a new creation (2 Corinthians 5:17)!

I praise you because I am fearfully and wonderfully made; your works are wonderful, I know that full well. — Psalm 139:14

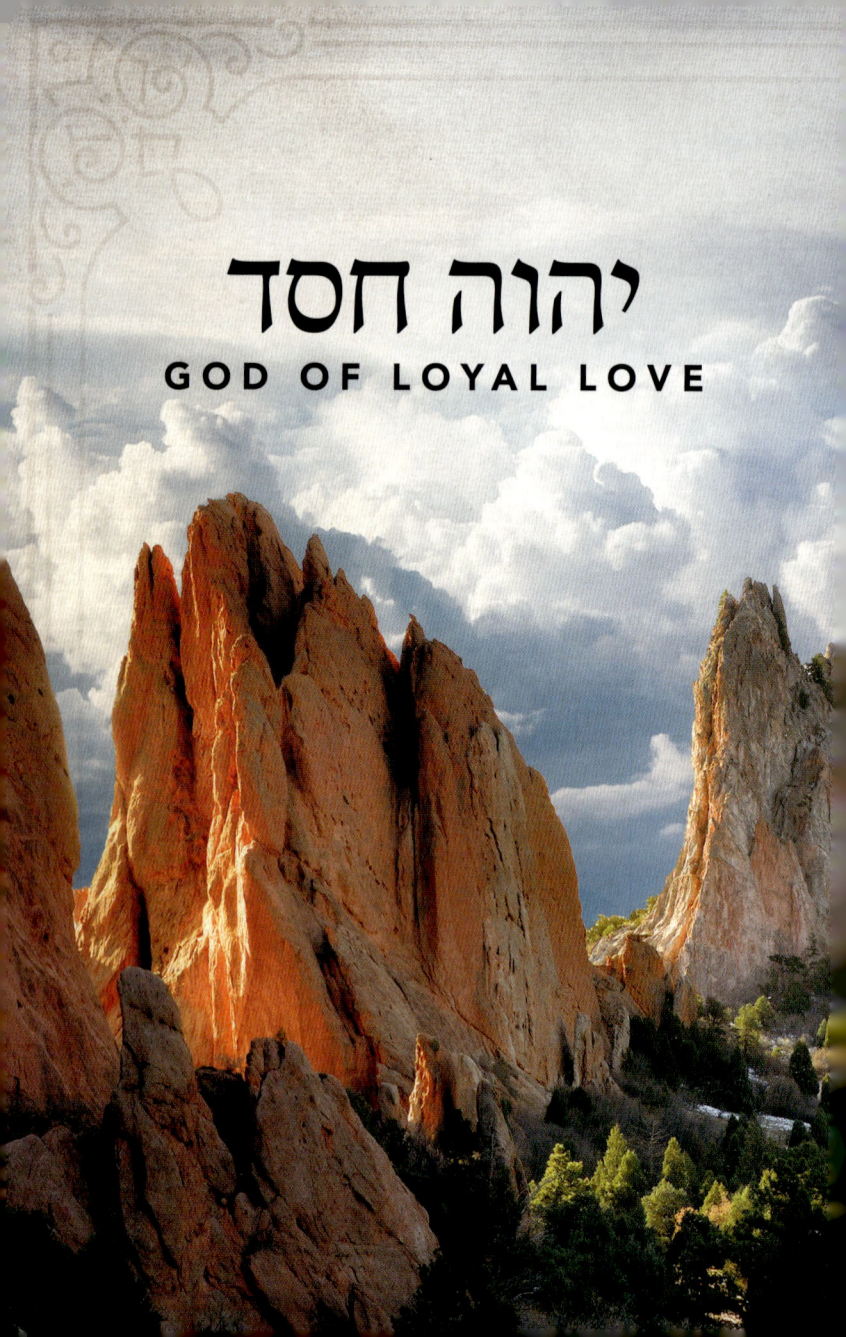

YAHWEH CHESED
GOD OF LOYAL LOVE

Do you understand God's love for you?

I once took a photo at a place called Garden of the Gods in Colorado Springs, Colorado. As I took the photo of a rock formation surrounded by the Rocky Mountains, a verse in the book of Isaiah came to mind: "Though the mountains be shaken and the hills be removed, yet my unfailing love for you will not be shaken" (Isaiah 54:10).

The Hebrew word for "love" in this verse is the word *hesed* or *checed* (חֶסֶד, pronounced "kheh-sed"), which is actually a hard word to translate into English.

Theologian John Oswalt says *chesed* is "a completely undeserved kindness and generosity." *Chesed* is not just a feeling; it's an action. It "intervenes on behalf of loved ones and comes to their rescue," according to author Lois Tverberg. *Chesed* is not romantic love. It's a faithful, reliable type of love.

It's a wife praying for years for her husband to know God. It's a dad once again bailing his drug-addicted son out of jail. It's a parent who lovingly cares daily for their autistic child. *Chesed* is faithful. *Chesed* is loyal. *Chesed* is love based in action.

And most importantly, *chesed* is the unfailing love God has for *you*, which is why God is known as the "God of Loyal Love"—*Yahweh Chesed*.

As pastor Rick Warren says, "God's love is like an ocean; you can see its beginning, but not its end."

Today, no matter what you face, you can rely on *Yahweh Chesed*.

"Though the mountains be shaken and the hills be removed, yet my unfailing love for you will not be shaken." — Isaiah 54:10

עמנו אל

GOD WITH US

EMMANUEL
GOD WITH US

Do you need God's presence today?

One morning I took a photo of El Capitan in Yosemite National Park. It was snowing, and the granite monolith was covered in fog. To get this photo, I had to wait for the snow to stop and then wait for the fog to clear so I could get a shot of the mountain.

While I had to wait to see this rock, have you ever considered that you *never* have to hunt for Jesus?

You see, one of the names for Jesus in Hebrew is *Emmanuel* (עמנו אל, pronounced "im-mah-nu-ale"), which literally means "I AM with you always."

And when you look deeper into the root of this Hebrew word, you discover that it doesn't just mean that Jesus is visiting with you or doing something with you—it means He is actually dwelling with you!

This name means that Jesus is always—*always*—with you because He never leaves you or forsakes you.

It means He is the Lord of your past, He is the Lord of your present moment right here and now, and He is the Lord of your future too.

This truth should give us comfort today, because as Christian speaker and actress Roma Downey says, "I am not afraid of tomorrow because I know God is already there." Or, as pastor Louie Giglio says, we are able to "start with Jesus, stay with Jesus, and end with Jesus" because He is with us always!

Whatever may happen throughout your day, do you trust that Jesus will be with you today?

And they shall name him Emmanuel, which means 'God is with us.
— Matthew 1:23 NRSV

אל חנון

THE GRACIOUS GOD

EL CHANNUN
THE GRACIOUS GOD

Have you ever screwed up?

Have you ever felt like you messed everything up? Like you said something or posted something that you deeply regret? Like you could never be forgiven for something you did?

If your answer to any of these questions is yes, I want you to know that you're not alone. In fact, if screw-ups were pull-ups, I'd be pretty ripped.

But through experience I've learned that the best way of letting go of past mistakes is to understand the power of God's grace.

The Hebrew word we translate in the Bible as "grace" is *chen* (חן, pronounced "khane"), which means "to show mercy," "unmerited favor," or "acceptance." So, when God shows us grace, He is accepting us into His family with unmerited favor—regardless of what we've done, said, or posted on social media!

And the good news is that despite our mistakes, God's grace never runs out! In fact, one of my favorite names for God in the Bible is *El Channun* (חנון אל, pronounced "el khan-noon"), which translates as "The Gracious God." This name indicates that God is always inviting, and re-inviting, us into His family.

Author Bob Goff says, "Grace is like the sunrise: it's there for us every day whether we choose to enjoy it or not." Perhaps this explains why I love photographing sunrises, like one that I took on the shore of the Sea of Galilee, because I always need to be reminded of God's grace through Jesus when I repent and turn back to Him.

Am I the only one who needs this reminder today?

But grace was given to each one of us according to the measure of Christ's gift. — Ephesians 4:7 ESV

האל הנאמן

THE FAITHFUL GOD

EL HANNE'EMAN
THE FAITHFUL GOD

Why do you say "Amen" after a prayer?

This is a word we all use often, but do you know what the word *amen* means?

In English, *amen* has basically come to mean "we're finished praying so we can all open our eyes." In Hebrew, however, *amen* (אמן, pronounced "ah-mane" or "ah-men") is actually a collection of several words that mean "trustworthy," "true," "firm," "reliable," and, most of all, "faithful."

So, one of the reasons we say "amen" is to be reminded that God is reliable, that God is faithful. It reminds us that he is trustworthy and faithful and can be counted on to respond to our prayers. In fact, one of the Hebrew names for God we find in Scripture is *El Hanne'eman* (האל הנאמן, pronounced "El Hahn-ay-aw-mane"), which means "The Faithful God."

This name even includes the Hebrew word for "amen" in it!

It reminds me of the words of pastor Louie Giglio, who says, "If only we knew what was happening when we pray, we would never cease to pray."

And since in Hebrew *amen* is used as a verb more than one hundred times in the Bible, saying it at the end of a prayer is a way of reminding ourselves that God is trustworthy, true, and reliable. When we say amen after praying with someone, it should not just be used as a way to passively agree with that prayer, but as an acknowledgment that we are trusting our faithful God together.

So, what are you doing today to be the answer to someone's prayers?

Know therefore that the LORD your God is God; he is the faithful God, keeping his covenant of love to a thousand generations of those who love him and keep his commandments. — Deuteronomy 7:9

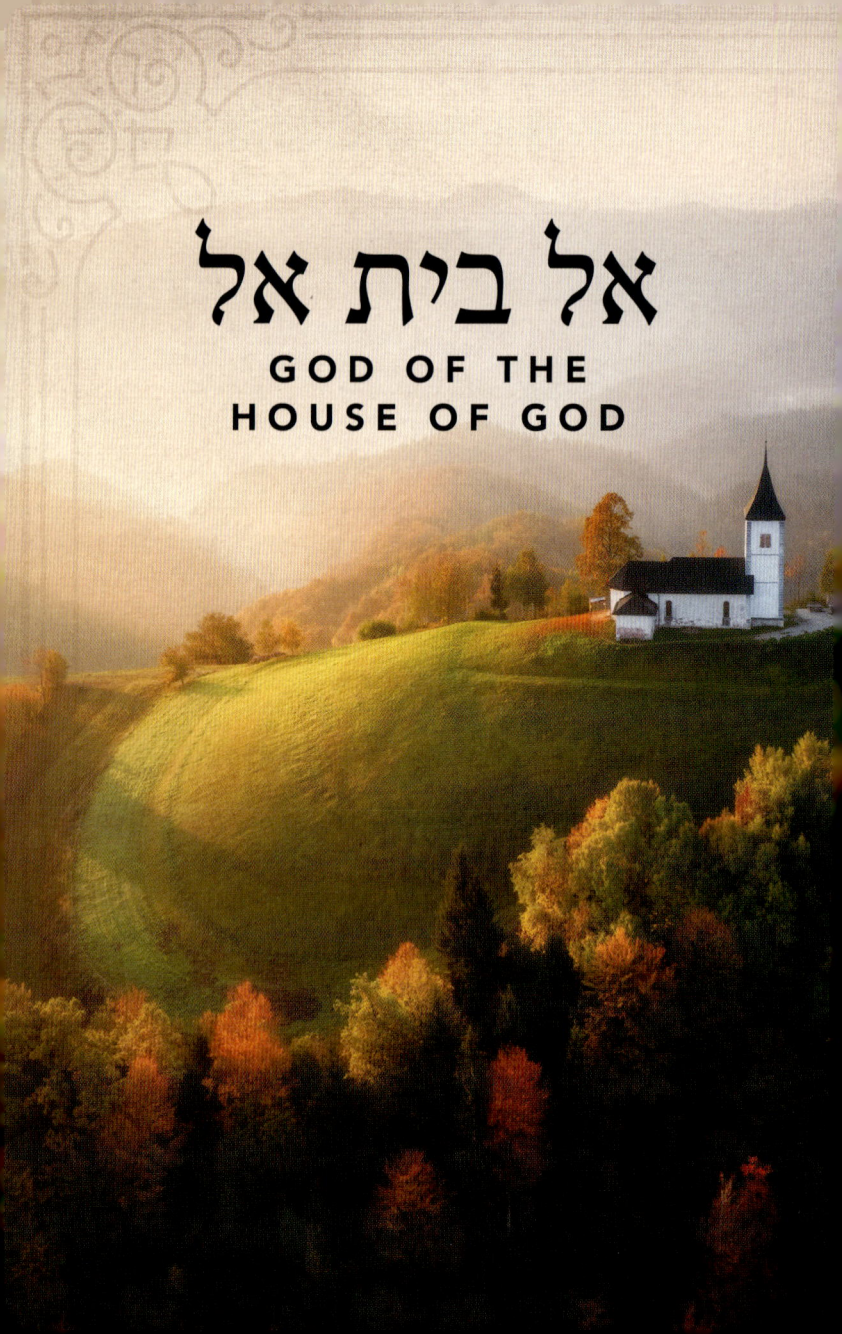

אל בית אל

GOD OF THE
HOUSE OF GOD

EL BETHEL
GOD OF THE
HOUSE OF GOD

Do you know God's address?

Today, the ancient Temple Mount in Jerusalem, near the top of Mount Moriah, is the location of the Dome of the Rock, but in the time of Jesus it was the place where the Holy of Holies stood.

To this day, this place is considered one of the most holy places on earth for Christians, Jews, and Muslims. But the Temple Mount is not a holy place because of its location in Jerusalem—it's holy because God once dwelt there.

You see, the believers of Jesus' day understood that God chose to be present in the Temple in Jerusalem. This is where people could come to meet with Him.

The first time in Scripture that God is considered to dwell in a specific place happens when Jacob meets with God one night, and in the morning builds a memorial to God and calls it "Bethel," which means "the house of God" (Genesis 28:18–19). He later called it "El Bethel" because the place was not as important as the God of the place. This word, *El Bethel* (אל בית אל, pronounced "El Bet-el"), means "God of the House of God."

More than a thousand years later, on the day Christians call Pentecost, one of Jesus' followers named Luke writes in Acts chapter 2 that by the Holy Spirit God is present with each believer.

This led Paul, one of the first followers of Jesus, to write that "you are God's temple" (1 Corinthians 3:16 ESV). You are a symbol of *Bethel*, and the Spirit of *El Bethel* dwells in you!

And the people around you will know you are a temple of the Holy Spirit by the words you choose, by the actions you take, and by the hope that you live with.

It is no longer I who live, but Christ lives in me. — Galatians 2:20 NLT

ADON HA'ADONIM
LORD OF LORDS

Why is Jesus Lord?

The title of "LORD" is one of the most commonly used in the Bible when referring to God. It's so common that we often overlook the fact that this is also one of the most important names of God found in the Bible.

You see, in Hebrew, this word is *Adonai*, which refers to a sovereign ruler, master, or controller.

The author of the book of Revelation takes this word a step further, referring to Jesus as the "Lord of lords," which in Hebrew is *Adon ha'adonim* (האדונים אדון, pronounced "ad-oneha-ah-do-nim"). The idea is that Jesus is the supreme authority in the world!

Jesus Himself said that He had been given all authority on heaven and on earth (Matthew 28:18), which means He has authority over all rulers, presidents, prime ministers, monarchs, magistrates, politicians, legislators, judges, authorities, managers, bosses, and every other imaginable type of leader!

And yet this Jesus, the Lord of lords, has declared His love for you—and calls you *friend*!

Which is why the late pastor Tim Keller said, "Jesus is all you need." It's also why actress Danica McKeller can say only Jesus can bring "absolute joy and freedom," and her friend Candace Cameron Bure can say that "Jesus is enough."

Yes. Yes He is.

On his robe and on his thigh he has a name written, King of kings and Lord of lords. — Revelation 19:16 ESV

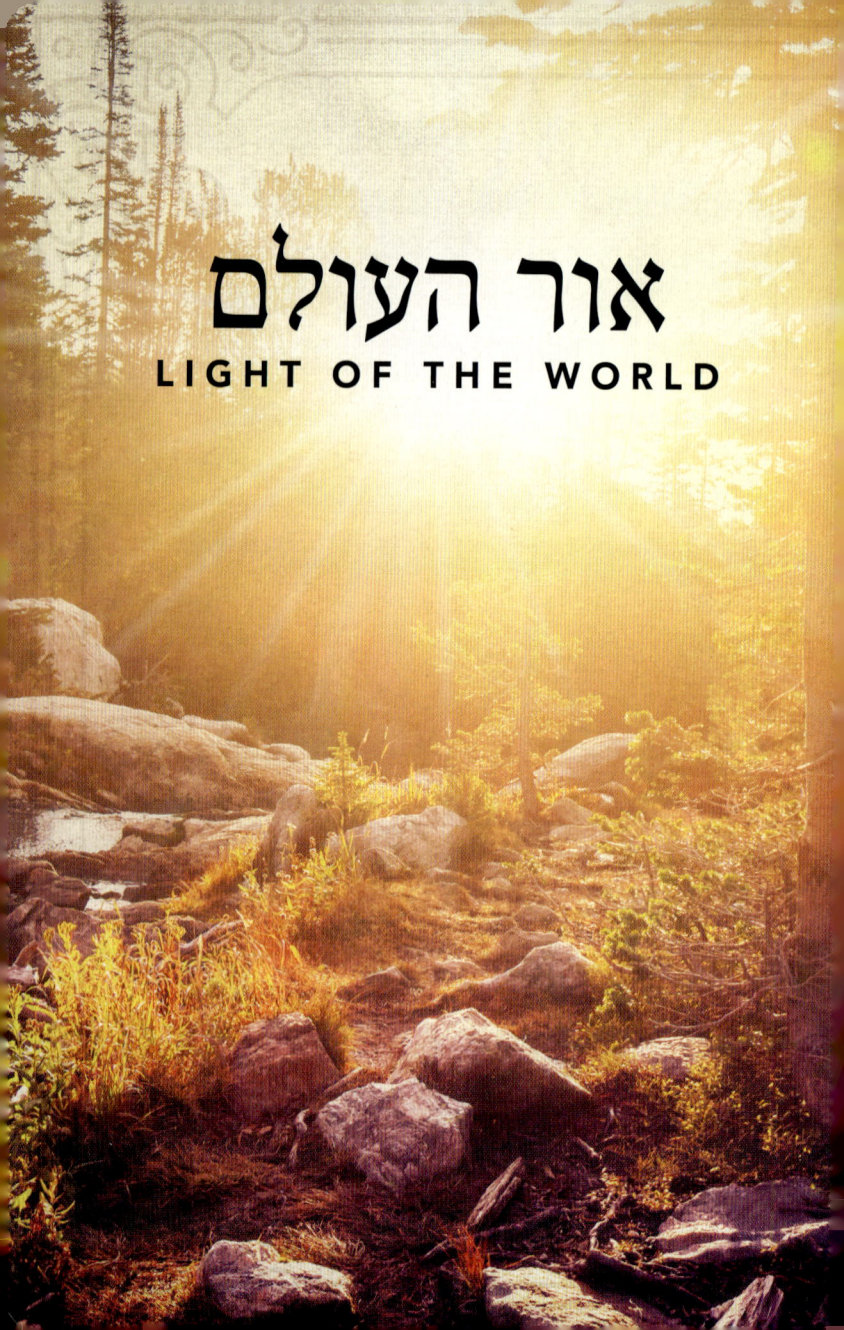

OHR HAOLAM
LIGHT OF THE WORLD

Do you shine brightly for God?

Do you know what Jesus meant when He said His followers would be "full of light" when they show compassion to people in need?

Jesus wasn't pushing a New Age agenda when He said His followers would be "full of light." He was explaining that taking care of people in need was not just a nice habit to have or a suggestion.

Compassion is supposed to be a central character trait of anyone who claims to be a follower of Jesus.

You see, the Hebrew word we translate as "light" is *owr* or *ohr* (אור, pronounced "ore"), which can also mean to shine. It's interesting that when God said "Let there be light" in the Creation story, He brought order to chaos. And when followers of Jesus bring order to people who are facing chaos or are hurting or in need, that's when our light shines before others!

When compassion for others is a central part of who we are as believers, that's when our bodies are full of light. That's when we shine brightly in a dark world and bring glory to God.

And Jesus personified this idea, even calling Himself the "Light of the World"—*Ohr HaOlam* (אור העולם, pronounced "ore Ha-oh-lam").

In so many ways, our world is in chaos right now. Imagine if five years from now, when the world looks back on this time, people could say that while they may not agree with what we believe about Jesus, that Christians were the most compassionate, generous, hope-filled people in the community!

So, are you ready to shine God's light into the world by being compassionate, generous, and hopeful today?

If you are filled with light, with no dark corners, then your whole life will be radiant, as though a floodlight were filling you with light.
— Luke 11:36 NLT

שַׂר שָׁלוֹם

PRINCE OF PEACE

SAR SHALOM
PRINCE OF PEACE

Where do you find peace?

We live in a world that can often seem increasingly void of peace. Depression, anxiety, social and political turmoil, fear, and anger are commonplace. So where do you go in search of peace?

Long before Jesus was born, the Hebrew prophet Isaiah declared that the coming Messiah would be known as the Prince of Peace. In Hebrew, this title is *Sar Shalom* (שׂר שׁלום, pronounced "sar shah-lome"), which is formed from two Hebrew words: *sar*, meaning "chief," "captain," or "leader"; and *shalom*, which means "safety" and "completeness."

The mission Jesus had throughout His life was to lead a broken world to safety and wholeness—to be the person who completely restored and reconciled our relationship with God.

In His life and teachings, Jesus personified the peace of God by showing us how to live peacefully with God and with others.

He promised and taught us how to have peace with God, safety during the hard times of life, security in times of stress, and hope in times of anxiety. This is why He is worthy of the name "Prince of Peace."

Jesus as the Prince of Peace is the antidote to the busyness, polarization, and fear that is prevalent in our world.

No matter what you're facing today, whether it's broken relationships, loneliness, depression, sickness, or stress, Jesus offers to lead you to peace.

And he will be called: Wonderful Counselor, Mighty God, Everlasting Father, Prince of Peace. — Isaiah 9:6 NLT

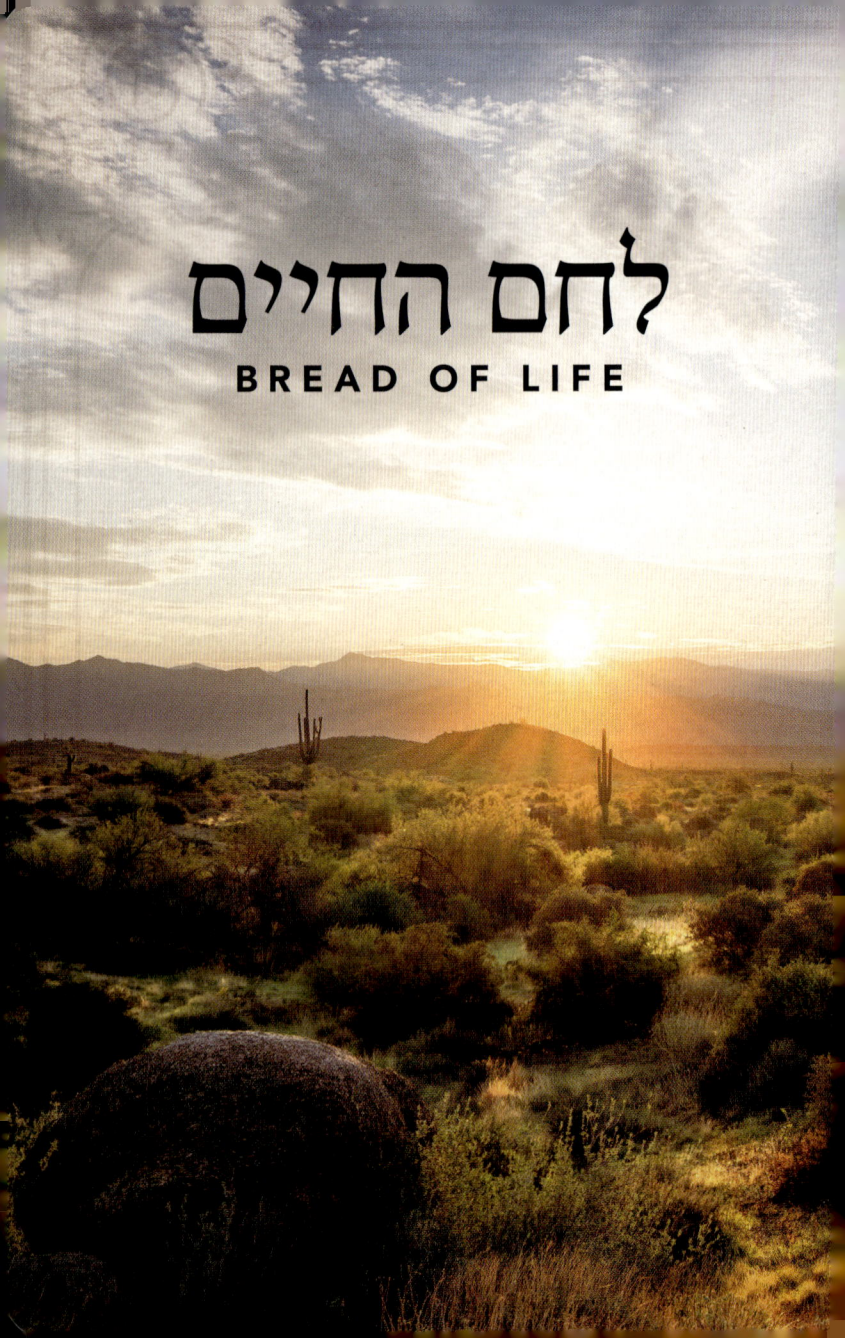

לחם החיים
BREAD OF LIFE

LECHEM
HA-CHAYIM
BREAD OF LIFE

There are a lot of cultural and historical insights into the birth of Jesus that we often miss as western Christians.

For example, we often think there were three wise men at the birth of Jesus, but the Gospels only state that there were three *gifts*. Historically, the Magi traveled as part of a large caravan—up to twenty or more—because they were traveling with valuables like gold, frankincense, and myrrh. And on top of this, they weren't at Jesus' birth, but arrived much later (Matthew 2:1 says they went to Jerusalem first).

And while nearly all Christians are likely to know that Jesus was born in Bethlehem, there is something about this you may not be aware of.

You see, the word *Bethlehem* is actually made up of two Hebrew words. The first is *bet* (בית, pronounced "beth"), which means "house," and the second is *lechem* (לחם, pronounced "lekh-em"), which means "bread." So, *Bethlehem* literally means "house of bread."

But why is this important?

Well, Jesus declared that He was the Bread of Life, the *Lechem Ha-Chayim* (לחם החיים, pronounced "lekh-em ha-khah-yim"), which was a reference to Him being the manna—the bread from heaven that fed the Israelites in the desert during the exodus. And His birth in Bethlehem means the Bread of Life was born in the house of bread!

Everything about the historical, cultural Christmas story is filled with Jesus—including the meaning of the name of the place where Jesus was born.

For unto you is born this day in the city of David a Savior, who is Christ the Lord. — Luke 2:11 ESV

משיח

MESSIAH

MASHIACH
MESSIAH

Have you heard Jesus' first sermon?

The first recorded sermon Jesus ever gave was just nine words long.

He read from chapter 61 in the book of Isaiah about the role of the Messiah, which in Hebrew is *Mashiach* (משיח, pronounced "maw-shee'-akh"). Jesus then simply preached these words: "Today this scripture is fulfilled in your hearing." His message may have been short, but those nine words can have a profound impact on your life—if you understand them.

You see, the Isaiah passage Jesus read describes how the Messiah would bring "good news" to the poor, restore the brokenhearted, and comfort those who mourn. The Hebrew word we translate as "good news" in Isaiah 61:1 is *besorah* (בשורה, pronounced "be-sow-rah"), which means news that is life changing.

Isaiah specifically wrote that the Messiah would bring *besorah* that would set people free and transform them into "oaks of righteousness" who would reveal God's splendor!

So, when Jesus said He had "fulfilled" these words, He was saying that everyone who follows Him is free from whatever has been holding them back or keeping them captive. This means *you* are free! You are now an oak of righteousness displaying God's glory!

Some California oak trees are more than eighty feet tall. They stand tall and strong because their roots are deep and their foundation is solid. Such trees are a picture of all of us who follow Jesus—you have everything you need to stand strong like these oak trees, no matter what you're facing!

And that's why Jesus' first sermon is life changing for you, because it means you have been set free. As pastor Judah Smith has said, "Our righteousness doesn't depend on our present performance but on Jesus' finished performance." That's the good news in Jesus' first message!

So, will you live in this freedom today?

They will be called oaks of righteousness, a planting of the LORD for the display of his splendor. — Isaiah 61:3

גּוֹאֵל

REDEEMER

GOEL
REDEEMER

Do you know Jesus' favorite book in the Torah?

In the four Gospels, Jesus quotes more often from the book of Deuteronomy than any other book in the Torah, which are the first five books of the Bible.

But do you know what the word *Deuteronomy* even means?

Well, in English it comes from a Greek word meaning "copy of the law," which makes sense when you consider that a large portion of the book is a speech made by Moses, where he reiterates the laws God had laid out for his people. But the Hebrew word for the book of Deuteronomy is *Devarim* (דברים, pronounced "de-vah-reem"), which means "words."

This Hebrew title, like all the other books of the Torah, comes from the first sentence in Deuteronomy, which reads, "These are the words Moses spoke to all Israel in the wilderness."

So, why is this Jesus' favorite book?

I think part of the reason is that in Deuteronomy, Moses reminds the people of Israel how God redeemed them from slavery in Egypt. This is Moses' final message—that God is the Redeemer.

The Hebrew word we translate as "redeemer" is *goel* (גואל, pronounced "goh-el"), which means "to buy back," which is what Jesus' life was about. The Apostle Paul, one of the earliest followers of Jesus, made this clear when he when he wrote that Jesus "purchased our freedom and forgave our sins" (Colossians 1:14 NLT).

Your life was redeemed when Jesus paid the price on the cross to set you free from sin!

And this means that no matter what you've been through, what you've done, or what you're facing, God can redeem your story—it's what He does.

He wants to speak words to you in your wilderness, and today I'm praying that you hear Him.

God bought you with a high price. So you must honor God with your body. — 1 Corinthians 6:20 NLT

רבי

TEACHER

RABBI
TEACHER

Do you ever doubt Jesus?

Around the world, the place of authority in a city or town is usually a beautiful, ornate city-hall building. Philadelphia's City Hall—one of my favorites—has a thirty-seven-foot statue of the city founder, William Penn, on top.

But did you know that in the Bible, authority was not found in a building, but in a person? Let me explain.

Jesus was often called "rabbi" in Hebrew (רבי, pronounced "ra-bee"), which means "my teacher." But there were two types of rabbis in ancient Israel: first, there were rabbis who taught the Hebrew Bible and were called "teachers of the law," and then there were a rare few who had such a deep understanding of Scripture that they had authority to introduce new interpretations.

After the time when the Bible was written, rabbis used the Hebrew word *s'mikhah* or *semikhah* (סמיכה, pronounced "shme-kah") for "authority." This was even the title given to a small number of rabbis in Jewish history. Jesus was truly a rabbi with authority.

While Jesus' first followers, the religious leaders, and even a Roman centurion recognized Jesus' authority, many people still questioned Him. They didn't believe He was who He claimed to be. I wonder how many of you reading this today also have doubts about Jesus' authority.

Maybe you follow Jesus, but you still have doubts. You want to be strong in your faith, but you're facing a desperate situation that has caused you to question whether Jesus can get you through it.

If that's you today, then I just want to remind you that Jesus gave His power and authority to His followers—He passed down His *s'mikhah* to you!

This means you have the authority, through Jesus, to deal with whatever situation you're facing today! When Jesus has authority over your life, you have authority to get through life—no matter what it throws at you!

One day Jesus called together his twelve disciples and gave them power and authority. — Luke 9:1 NLT

NECHAMA
GOD OF ALL COMFORT

Do you ever feel like you need a break?

We are living in a time of heightened fear and anxiety in the world, and I sure feel it. We live in a time when everyone seems rushed and busy, and when increased religious, political, and social polarization is causing relationships to be tense or even fractured.

I feel them despite having faith in a God who is described as "the God of all comfort, who comforts us in all our troubles" (2 Corinthians 1:3-4).

This verse was written in Greek, but it is the equivalent of the Hebrew word *nechamah* (נחמה, pronounced "nekh-aw-maw") which means to "bring rest." The idea is that even in the middle of extreme chaos, people of faith can find rest in knowing that God is in control.

I bet everyone reading these words today could use some more rest and comfort, right!

Jesus, who personified the comfort of God, made His home base in Capernaum on the shore of the Sea of Galilee during his ministry. *Capernaum* is made up of two Hebrew words, *kfar nahum*. This combination of words means the "village of comfort."

So, the God of all comfort, who comforts each of us in our troubles, stepped into history as Jesus, and lived in the village of comfort!

Today, my prayer is that you would find comfort and rest in knowing that God is in control.

Your promise revives me; it comforts me in all my troubles.
— Psalm 119:50 NLT

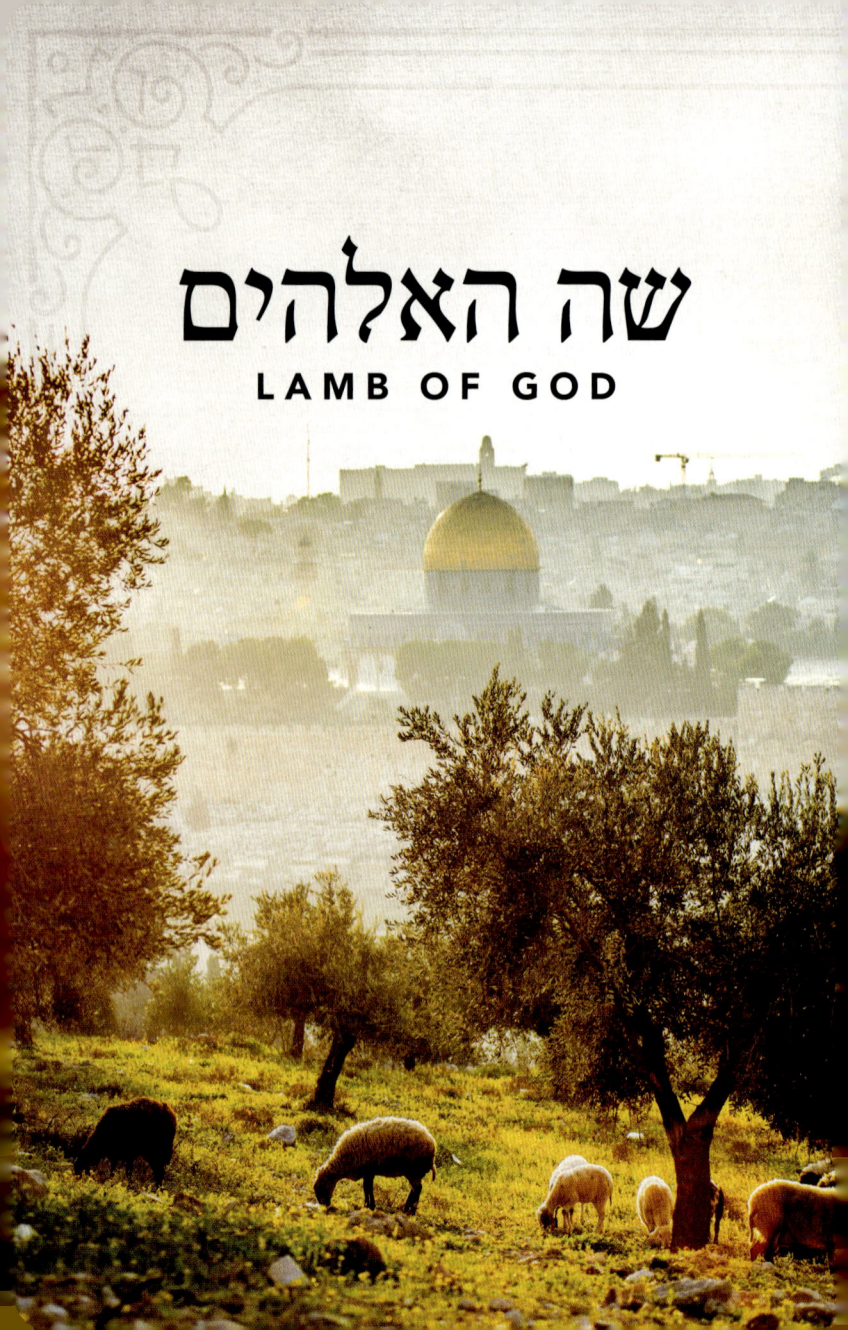

SEH HAELOHIM
LAMB OF GOD

Want a new take on Palm Sunday?

Church tradition says that on Palm Sunday, Jesus entered Jerusalem through the Golden Gate, which is also known as the Gate of Mercy. This was the gate kings would use to enter the Holy City at the time of Jesus.

It makes sense that the King of kings would go through this gate into Jerusalem during the triumphal entry, right?

But Jesus didn't arrive in Jerusalem on just any day. He arrived four days before the Passover—a day known as Lamb Selection Day. On this day, Jewish families went to the Temple to select and purchase the lamb that would be their Passover sacrifice, which in Hebrew is *Korban Pesakh* (קרבן פסח, pronounced "kor-bawn peh'-sakh").

Jewish law required that the lambs at the Temple come from the fields of nearby Bethlehem, and to make access easy for the thousands of lambs coming into the city for Passover, a sheep gate was built, according to Nehemiah 3, that was right near the Temple.

This sheep gate is now called the Lions' Gate.

So, what if Jesus made a right turn at the gate fit for a king to instead enter by the nearby sheep gate? After all, Jesus was entering Jerusalem not to receive a crown but to become our sacrifice!

Wouldn't it have been fitting for Jesus to go through the sheep gate? I mean, He was called the Lamb of God, which in Hebrew is *Seh HaElohim* (שה האלהים, pronounced "see Ha-el-oh-heem").

Jesus, the Lamb of God, born in Bethlehem, going through the sheep gate on the day lambs were selected for the forgiveness of sin is an interesting scenario to imagine.

Even more amazing is the fact that Jesus, the Lamb of God, was willing to be sacrificed in our place so that we could be set free from sin and welcomed into a relationship with God forever!

Look, the Lamb of God, who takes away the sin of the world! — John 1:29

This book is the second in a series by Dave Adamson.
If you have enjoyed it, check out his first book, which has sold over
100,000 copies, *52 Hebrew Words Every Christian Should Know.*

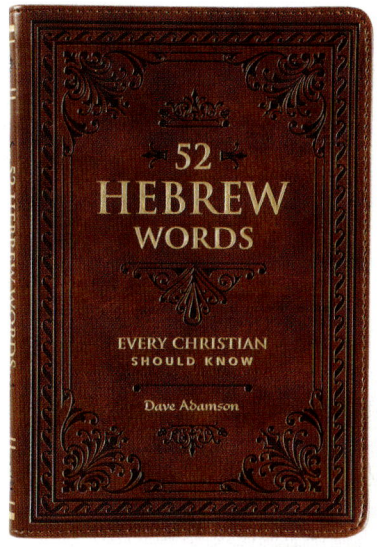

For more information about this or other Christ-centered
devotionals and gift books, visit www.christianartgifts.com.

NOTES

_____

_____

_____

_____

_____

_____

_____

_____

_____

_____

_____

_____